How To Win At Life And Love

A 14-STEP GUIDE TO ATTRACT, WIN, AND KEEP THE PARTNER OF YOUR DREAMS

Allon Khakshouri

PRAISE FOR

HOW TO WIN AT LIFE AND LOVE

"This is a very engaging and insightful read. The author is a leading sports agent - having represented some of the top tennis players in the world, including Novak Djokovic. He has, through an understanding and application of Sam Kogan's life changing 'The Science of Acting', along with other fascinating insights into human consciousness and behavior, written a compelling step-by-step guide to creating a loving and lasting relationship.

Thoroughly recommend - and not to just those who are looking for that special someone!"

Neil Sheffield
Actor, Principal at Kogan Academy of Dramatic Arts

"Allon Khakshouri has written a clear, insightful book on personal peak performance derived from his professional experience as a world-class tennis promoter. Filled with anecdotes from the world of elite tennis, Engaged chronicles his parallel journey to a fulfilling relationship through mindful self-improvement. A must-read for anyone learning how to love. Definitely recommend!"

Nelson Moussazadeh
Book Reader/Reviewer

"Engaged is an excellent and thought-provoking book about working out who you really are and how you can best express it. It looks at how the subconscious thoughts that we have developed over a lifetime create a king of 'groove' into which we can get stuck, and suggests the best ways to drag ourselves back out of that groove. Khakshouri describes a number of techniques, largely based on acting theory, which can be used to develop new kinds of thinking that will replace the unhelpful previous thoughts. It could take a lifetime to put all of these ideas fully into practice, but this book makes an interesting case

for doing so. It's certainly given me some things to think about, and I recommend it."

Steven Heywood
Freelance Writer, Editor and Researcher

"Very honest and authentic read. The author describes his personal journey in a very genuine manner, not glossing over his own shortcomings, and always focusing on what he learned from them. I also liked how he juxtaposes his professional success managing some of the world's premier athletes with his personal challenges to find his own inner happiness. A well-written personal story that touches on many universal themes."

Rabin Y
Book Reader/Reviewer

"Personal stories of the author make it an easy and an exciting read. The book includes many advices that can trigger personal growth and development. We often get influenced by the opinions of others so much that we forget about what is best for us. In order to attract the person of your dreams you have to start by working on yourself first. I highly recommend this book to people who are trying to find themselves and a lifetime companion."

Sabina A.
Book Reader/Reviewer

"Why on earth wasn't this book published 10 years ago?! I could have saved myself so much stress.

It contains many fascinating insights into the human condition. The author has utilized a wide range of sources and studies to illustrate his points. everything he says is backed up by some authority or other, which makes a pleasant change from many of the personal development books I have read. he uses a simple and very readable structure, and I particularly enjoyed the little touches like the very apt quotes that litter the book throughout.

the book is split into two parts - and it's the second that really grabbed my attention; it is a step-by-step guide to get into, and maintain a fulfilled relationship. I can't think of anyone I know that couldn't do with some guidance in this area.

I am looking forward to reading the next book by this author, and would recommend this book to anyone who wants to improve the quality of their life using a clear step by step process."

James Whittaker
Book Reader/Reviewer

"I heard about this book from a friend. It's well written and very authentic. A very insightful read. Definitely recommend."

KatrinYaghoubi
Founder / President: Rondeel Research Group

"Although I've already found the love of my life and have been happily married for over a year, the author has brought out some important points in this book to help me nurture and grow my ever budding marriage. I highly recommend this book to not only readers who are looking to find the right one, but also a reader who is interested in further strengthening their relationship."

David M.
Book Reader/Reviewer

"This is without a doubt the easiest to read relationship book I have ever read. A lot of other books (I won't name names) just offer shortcuts to attraction, but Engaged actually gets at the core issue: thoughts and behaviors.

It is an easy read, a fascinating read, and, most importantly, a useful read!"

Maria Bertorelli
Book Reader/Reviewer

Special Gifts for Readers:

As a reader of this book, you can get free access to the detailed training that walks you through these 14 steps in detail.

Please visit the following site to get instant access to:
allonkhakshouri.com/free

This book is dedicated to all the single people of this world who, like me, wish for nothing more than to be in a happy relationship, or even to be married with kids.

WHY THIS BOOK IS
SO IMPORTANT FOR YOU

Having been the agent of some of the world's most successful tennis players including world #1 Novak Djokovic, one of my biggest interests has always been trying to understand what drives people and makes them performat their best. What separates the champions from the runners up? When the difference in ability amongst the top players is negligible, what is that key ingredient that helps one athlete consistently win at the highest level, while another consistently fails? At the same time that I explored these questions for others, I was failing at what seemed most important for the success and happiness of my own life—my personal quest to find the perfect woman I would want to share my life with.

I remember the painful feeling of being unable to attract a lasting relationship despite considering myself a good catch. I worked on my looks, at being professionally successful, and anything else I believed would make a difference. But nothing seemed to help. Secretly, I was envying those friends of mine who seemed to get every girl they wanted. I just couldn't understand why it was so hard for me to find lasting love. Life seemed so unfair to me. This was until I finally undertook the steps that I will share with you in this book, and which have transformed my life.

Finding true love is critical. Most of our happiness comes from our relationships with other people. Research has shown on numerous occasions that married people live a healthier life physically and spiritually, recover better from diseases, and live a healthier lifestyle. According to an article from Harvard Health Publications, a survey of 127,545 men proved that married men live longer than single, divorced or widowed men.

A recent study by the American College of Cardiology's 63rd Annual Scientific Session found that married men have lower rates of several cardiovascular diseases compared to single, divorced, and widowed men. In the National Longitudinal Mortality Study published in 2000 by the US Census Bureau, 281,460 men and women aged 45 and older were compared with regard to mortality.

The finding was that unmarried persons aged between 45- 64 years had a significantly higher risk of mortality than married people. Similar work conducted by the British Regional Heart Study, published in 1995, also found that being single was associated with an increased risk of death from a cardiovascular disease. And a 2013 study by Duke

University Medical Center in Durham, North Carolina, found that married people, in general, are half as likely to die during middle age as single people. In short, it seems that relationships are a crucial element for being happy and healthy, as they enrich our lives emotionally, connect us to others socially, and provide for much more mental stimulation.

But for many, the quest to find love seems so challenging. I remember how frustrated I was about not finding my perfect match, while at the same time hoping that some day the perfect partner would magically knock at my door and ask me to marry her. As time passed, I started feeling anxious about this dream not happening, and felt the pain of possibly never finding a soul mate to share my life with. Although it's never impossible, I now know from my own experience that as time passes, it becomes much harder to change our lives. Past experiences—through the mental processes that you will understand more as you read this book—engrain the habits that continue to determine our life script. This is what keeps us where we are, and makes change so difficult—unless we understand how we think, become aware of why we think as we do, and learn to change these patterns. This insight may be a huge disappointment to many. We have all become accustomed to the fast pace and quick fixes of our generation, insisting that short cuts can and should work. Sadly, however, when it comes to love, this form of laziness does not work well.

In hindsight, I now know that being single for so long can also be a huge opportunity. I have learned from the world of sport that it is the mindset of continuous learning that characterizes the very best. High performers believe that through hard work and self-correction, they can achieve anything they desire, and they use their heart and mind to succeed. Through sustained engagement with their goals, they not only respond to challenges, but also choose the changes they want to make in order to be successful. This is how they push themselves to fulfill their potential.

By maintaining sustained engagement with my goal of finding and keeping my dream partner, I also experienced massive breakthroughs in various areas of my life. From the moment that I envisioned the desire to find lasting love as an opportunity to also grow as a human being; my quest became a turning point in my life. In this process, I met the wife who has enriched my life so dramatically, but also learned more about myself, life, and people in one year than I had gathered throughout the entire rest of my life. I now want more than anything to take this opportunity to share with you, and as many people as possible, the knowledge I discovered that transformed my life so positively.

Throughout this process, I also learned that our brain is the most amazing gift we have, and it can help us achieve anything to which we aspire. The only problem is that it doesn't come with a user guide. In contrast to animals that rely on quick instincts and fast reactions, our brain can help us creatively map out a plan to achieve future goals. In fact, humans spend more time than any other creature as defense less infants in order to allow our brain to fully develop, and recent research has concluded that even as adults our brain is still able to evolve.

In short, knowledge based on the truth of how we think, and therefore how we live, is vital. Only with such awareness can we develop the skill to change, where necessary, our patterns of thinking to ones that are more conducive to achieving a fulfilled and happy life. We need to be able to learn how to create a mind that is sensitive and agile enough to be able to deal with whatever life throws, or has thrown, at us. We often carry around with us an invisible baggage of thoughts about ourselves, people, and life in general, and if we don't learn how to see and correctly address these thoughts, they can dictate our life and our perception of our free will without us even realizing.

However, the key to finding love is to be engaged to people, to life, and to one's self. Engaged here does not mean to connect to the pleasures of life in a merely consuming manner. Rather, I am referring to the kind of engagement whereby we are investing into our future, a form of flow that marks psychological growth. That is the meaning behind the title of this book. Obviously the ultimate aim of the book is to teach you how to create a life for yourself in which you will have the best chance of finding the partner of your dreams, and hopefully one day enjoying a happy engagement followed by a beautiful and long-lasting marriage. But the way in which we will reach that stage is by engaging with the patterns of thinking and the unconscious desires that we have developed over the course of a lifetime. It is through engaging critically and curiously with our internal workings that we can truly have an effect on our actions and on the external world, and achieve real psychological growth.

I am now convinced that learning how consciousness works in general, and then developing an awareness of our own patterns of thinking and how they have evolved is the most important skill we can learn to benefit our lives. It allows us to choose to think the thoughts that are in alignment with, and therefore help us achieve, the goals we set ourselves. In this book, I will share with you what I have learned about human thought, as well as revealing the step-by-step guide that has helped me to transform my life. While these steps may initially take some persistence to implement, I can promise you that they literally transformed my life within a year.

The alternative looks grave—simply continuing to do what you have already been doing, and hoping for a miracle. Based on what I witnessed among my many single friends, and up until recently have experienced for myself, this means focusing lots of energy on trying to find a partner, without taking the time to analyze why success is not forthcoming. Eventually, many people in this situation feel unbearable pressure from the perceived expectations of peers, friends, family, and society in general. Their only escape is to try to lose themselves to get away from the anticipation of living a lonely, unfulfilled life.

For some, this happens by simply focusing on one area of life, typically their work. Others lose themselves in specific thought patterns, and yet others may seek refuge in addictive and self-destructive habits. In most cases, I witness such friends living as slaves of time who resemble distracted animals that merely exist to survive. Sadly, they are likely to end up single for the rest of their lives, or to settle for relationships that are doomed to fail. In both cases, the result is suffering and a rapid erosion of their self-esteem.

Luckily, I found a way out of this horrible cycle. I believe we all deserve love, and I have come to understand that an important element to the meaning of our lives is found in the relationships we have with one another. I feel obligated to share my story and the steps that helped me enjoy the most loving relationship I could have imagined. While I can only say what worked for me, I hope my story will, at the very least, inspire you to take steps to reach for what ever you desire. Staying single can become a self-fulfilling prophecy of misery. At the same time, becoming the kind of person who attracts lasting relationships can propel us to success in other areas as well. Within this spirit, I hope that my book will encourage you to take action so that you will find the partner of your dreams.

CONTENTS

Introduction 1

PART ONE: UNDERSTANDING WHY YOU'RE SINGLE 6

1. *Stepping Out Of Your Shadow* 8

2. *Making A Choice* 12

3. *The Biggest Lessons of Life* 18

4. *Mental Laws To Success* 22

5. *The Science Of Acting* 25

6. *How We Learn* 27

7. *Pain And Pleasure* 31

8. *Visible And Invisible Thoughts* 33

9. *Fear And Shame* 35

10. *Awareness And Self-Conditioning* 40

11. *Chamber Of Visible Thinking* 43

12. *The Philosophy Of Growth* 47

13. *Purposes* 51

14. *Resetting The Love Thermostat* 54

**PART TWO: STEP-BY-STEP GUIDE TO BEING IN A
FULFILLING RELATIONSHIP** 57

Step One – Decide to Live Your Dreams 60

Step Two – Commit To A Plan And Build Momentum 65

Step Three – Get Out Of Your Head 69

Step Four – Create A Strong Purpose Of Wanting A Relationship 71

Step Five – Frequent Repetitive Thinking 74

Step Six – Find A Trusted Person 78

Step Seven – Get Out Of Your Ditch 80

Step Eight – Create A Positive Self-Image 87

Step Nine – Become True Toward Yourself 92

Step Ten – Connect With Your Heart 96

Step Eleven – Social Learning 100

Step Twelve – Have Courage And Fun 105

Step Thirteen – Train Your Willpower Muscle 112

Step Fourteen – Become Unstoppable 117

About The Author 121

Bibliography 123

INTRODUCTION

*"Turn your face to the sunshine,
the shadows fall behind you."*

— **Maori proverb**

It feels like yesterday when I called my girlfriend and told her to be ready for a fun evening. I specifically mentioned that she should dress casually. I had booked a chef to set up a private table on the beach and prepare a gourmet dinner for just the two of us.

As we arrived at the remote location, my girl friend was becoming a little anxious about where I was taking her.

I stopped my car close to a cliff and, after taking a few steps, she saw some rose petals laid on the sand. We followed them and saw a beautifully set table surrounded by candle lights. She broke into tears. Later, I took her on a short walk and proposed. Both of us were overwhelmed. I still see her expression, which transformed from initial surprise, to tears of joy and happiness. Her trembling voice said yes, while we hugged each other, symbolizing that we would never let go again. Finally being engaged was the biggest moment I had ever experienced and the starting point of a joint life full of love and excitement.

Only a year earlier, this moment had seemed so distant. This made me think about what had changed. I realized that the main influences for me in finding a partner, and ultimately receiving a greater understanding of myself as a result of happiness and love, evolved in two stages.

The first stage came from my professional work, which has involved studying the habits of ultra-successful people, and also finding and developing special talents in sports. I managed some of the sport's greatest players, including world #1 Novak Djokovic. I have spent hundreds of hours studying these greats closely, as well as other ultra-successful people. What I have learned is that the best of the best don't purely rely on their natural abilities; rather, they continue striving to develop themselves at all times, demonstrating a willingness to face challenges with an agile mindset. They are fully engaged with what they do and continually work on bettering their skills. They combine self-awareness with the determination to develop themselves to achieve their personal goals. As a result, they see effort as a key part of the recipe for success and difficulties as an opportunity for growth.

This sounds so simple, yet when it came to my personal life, I just couldn't apply this wisdom. I considered any form of self-correction as an attack on my self-image and an admission that I was flawed. Any attempt to critically engage with my ways of thinking and my perception of myself, others, and the world around me was met with resistance, whether conscious or unconscious. This is why it took me up until my mid-thirties to apply the lessons from my research and experience in sport to my dating life.

Up until then, my rigid, unaware mindset controlled my life, my decisions, and therefore my experiences—like a precise thermostat that regulates the room temperature and ensures it remains perfectly consistent. This kept me within the comfort zone of being a 'happy' bachelor. These invisible patterns of thinking ensured that, regardless of my circumstances (after all, the lifestyle I led meant I was often surrounded by beautiful people and fancy parties), I would nevertheless stay away from intimate lasting relationships and remain alone.

The second trigger evolved once I came across a particular theory of acting which could be applied to my life. The theory (and the book based on it) is called The Science of Acting and I learned it from an acting school called The Kogan Academy of Dramatic Arts (formerly known as The Academy of the Science of Acting and Directing). For more information on this

2

wonderful organization, check out allonkhakhsouri.com/free. In short, the school teaches pupils their theory of how thinking works, and how we can change our thoughts, so that they can then take over the thoughts of their characters and act in the most convincing manner. Rather than just mimicking their roles, students learn to become aware of their thoughts and feelings, so that they can replace them with those of the role, when necessary.

I was instantly inspired by their work, and chose to take some classes on their theory, before applying them to my own thoughts. This was a game changer. Never before have I come across a theory that explains thinking with such simplicity, and provides the tools to witness and change the thoughts that run our lives. I will be discussing the method and the tools used to achieve these changes throughout the rest of the book.

When we're single, we often feel that we have less of a need to question ourselves and change – we feel like we're happy with the way we are, and have nobody specific that we're trying to improve ourselves for, so why go to the effort of changing our lives? Although I too thought in this way, deep down I felt extremely lonely. I had a hunch that life could be so much more colorful with a partner to share and somebody to love. This is why, eventually, I took the specific steps I will share in this book. They allowed me to attract my wife into my world and experience for the first time what it means to live a fulfilling life.

In part one of this book, I will demonstrate the lesson I learned that transformed my life—namely, that thoughts and feelings developed over time (and often originating from our childhood), can create invisible programs in our minds that will run (and very possibly ruin) our lives unless we become aware of the them. Some of these invisible patterns of thinking will serve us positively, but others will do the exact opposite, no matter what our conscious intentions are at the time. Unless we learn to become aware of them, they create programs in our head that run our lives on autopilot.

One of my own programs that I became aware of was set to keep me away from lasting relationships. By simply becoming aware of the previously invisible thoughts that were determining my actions, I triggered massive changes in my life. Therefore, this part of the book will focus on sharing my understanding of how such thinking works. In part two, I will show you a step-by-step guide of how I was able to reset my relationship thermostat toward attracting my wife and living in a fulfilled relationship.

A quick word of caution: it is a common mistake to assume that gradual change will only engender small, incremental results. My experience has shown me that what may seem slow and difficult at first will, at some point, transform into massive results. Let me explain. Over time, some of our thinking can become like a block of ice. Depending on our experiences and relationship to these experiences, this block of ice can freeze— among other things—our natural ability to attract love. I'm sure you've met or known of people who may have an extraordinary talent in one field but, in other fields like social skills, they're deprived.

Our thinking can be like a block of ice that has frozen our natural ability to attract our perfect partner. This block will remain the same, or may even get harder over time, if ignored. When we first start to heat it up, very little happens as the temperature gets higher one degree at a time. We may become discouraged and assume that the ice will never melt. Suddenly, however, when the ice reaches one degree above freezing, everything speeds up—soon the ice is completely melted, and we're now able to reprogram 1 our minds. The previous incremental work of heating the ice has helped to create the conditions for this sudden tipping point. This is how the miracle of compounding works.

But is compounding really a miracle? In fact, compounding is generating benefits from previous earnings. In terms of thinking, this means creating positive feedback. Our mental complexes, once set, work by themselves in a positive feedback loop in which thoughts lead to actions, which reinforce thoughts, which further influence our actions, and soon. If we have the right complexes in our heads that help us to improve our life, then the results and benefits will grow and grow. The opposite will happen if we have negative complexes like life is hard, people don't care, people are stupid. Once we believe that life is about learning and growing, we realize that we have unlimited potential to achieve the most incredible goals we may have. The key is to get started and to follow through!

My hope is that by reading this book, understanding how we think, and then discovering your own invisible thoughts that may be holding you back in many areas of your life, you will reconnect to the innate ability that allows you to attract the partner of your dreams. More importantly, I believe that by challenging your single status, you will learn valuable lessons about yourself and your life that will help you achieve other goals and make you a happier person. So come on, let's take this journey together, and break the wall that's blocking your way to your happiness. For I am with you every step of the way.

PART ONE
UNDERSTANDING WHY YOU'RE SINGLE

"In the end, people either have excuses or experiences, reasons or results, buts or brilliance. They either have what they wanted or they have a detailed list of all the rational reasons why not."

— Anonymous

In this part, I will help you understand about what's holding you back from being in a relationship.

We all have these common nagging fears that's keeping us from finding our one true love. And this is for that reason this book is written to help you understand the root cause of your fear.

Fear has its own purpose. It is meant to keep us safe. However, in a relationship, it is unfortunately keeping us from being committed to a loving relationship. Because this means that you need to be vulnerable.

You need to understand that if you want to have a lasting and loving relationship, you need to free yourself from the fear that's keeping you away from love.

I personally did free myself and was able to attract the woman of my dreams, which is my wife. Now it's your turn to abandon that fear and start engaging in a happy intimate relationship.

- I will help you attract not just any partner, but the one who is truly meant for you.

- I will help you to truly make yourself ready to commit to a long lasting relationship.

- And all you need to do to make your relationship last.

As I firmly believe, no one is destined to live alone...

1
STEPPING OUT OF
YOUR SHADOW

*"Even if you fall on your face, you're
still moving forward."*

— **Victor Kiam**

From my late teens on, I considered myself a great catch. After all, I had wealthy parents, went to good schools, took part in sports teams, was very social, and had successful jobs. I was even a legend in our local nightlife, always being invited to the hotspots and knowing the most attractive people. And yet, I was single most of the time. At first, I interpreted and rationalized to myself that I was enjoying my freedom, and I was convinced that someday my ideal partner would show up, and we would move joyfully and effortlessly into marriage. After all, this seemed be happening to many of my friends. But, suddenly, I turned thirty-three years old, and I was still single.

For the first time, the thought popped into my mind that I was unable to maintain a lasting intimate relationship, and that maybe there was something wrong with me. Maybe I would even remain single for the rest of my life, doomed to die alone. I was picturing myself at a mature age, possibly without parents, and with no one to share my feelings, experiences, and life. I had serious self-doubts about myself, and I felt devastated.

Despite my big dream to be happily married, I kept this desire a secret, as it would create too much pressure. People thought I had many girlfriends and simply didn't feel like committing. Only I knew that I was a lonely soul, missing the love that I was craving for. And I didn't want anyone else to find out. It reminded me of one of my clients, who played down his anxieties by staying out late before big tennis matches. By doing so, he gave the impression that he didn't really care that much if he won or lost, and this of course helped to take off lots of the pressure he was experiencing.

Similarly, I didn't accept any support from friends, and I refused to go on dates that were set up for me. I made it seem as if I had no desire to commit to a serious relationship, while the truth was that I was simply scared of messing up. I didn't dare ask out the women I really desired or that could have been great matches for me. I usually ended up dating random girls with whom I didn't really intend to build lasting relationships. The outcome was that I remained single because, without knowing it at the time, that was the outcome I invisibly desired and which my thought patterns were working toward.

 Friends kept nagging me about getting married, and nagging my parents as well, who felt terribly embarrassed that their son was not able to live his life according to their expectations. Everyone thought I was just having fun, which made me feel relieved, as this image concealed the reality that I was not single by choice. In fact, even I started to believe this narrative, and I did little to try to discover what it was within me that kept me away from long-term relationships.

At that time, I had no knowledge of why and how we think. I had no 'road map' to get myself out of the dark woods that I was living in, and I had too much fear of discovering what it was I was actually thinking about and wanting. At this stage, it is worth noting that during this time in my life, what I consciously wanted and what I subconsciously wanted to achieve were the exact opposite of each other (with the latter being invisible to me).

Consciously, all I thought I wanted was to be loved and to be in love; yet subconsciously, I wanted to be on my own.

Unfortunately, my invisible, subconscious will was by far the stronger and, without me knowing, I had already submitted to it. It may seem alien to you that we can think thoughts that we're not aware of, but I hope that from reading this book, contemplating the ideas, and watching the videos offered, you will have a greater understanding of how this is true, and what you need to change in your subconscious thinking to make yourself happier. One autumn, shortly before my 34th birthday, I met this gorgeous girl who was selling me a mobile phone subscription. I instantly fell for her and, after a few weeks, we ended up dating. I was convinced that she was finally the love of my life, the princess I had been waiting for all this time. All my friends loved her, and it made me feel so good to be going out with a superhot South-American-looking girl. We spent many fun days partying together, getting drunk, and getting to know each other a little better. I enjoyed so much social proof with her as my girlfriend, and that made me feel extremely good. Nobody could suspect my insecurities about women—not even myself! Although she barely spoke English, and it was very hard to communicate, I was convinced that my princess had finally shown up.

But then, as suddenly as she had entered my life, she disappeared. I was shocked. I felt so much pain. Suddenly, all my doubts reemerged, together with my fear of permanent loneliness. I couldn't understand what had happened. In that moment, I knew that I had reached the crossroads: I could keep doing what I had been doing and living the illusion of being a womanizer while suffering from terrible loneliness, or I could do whatever it would take to find a companion for life. The first choice would mean living within my comfort zone and probably remaining single for the rest of my life. The second one could mean learning lessons from the past by dedicating myself to the truth, and then taking action.

Although being on my own caused such stress and suffering, my first step in becoming aware of my consciousness, and therefore how I lived, was to understand that I was single because I wanted to be. This was a hard pill to swallow, as it was the exact opposite to what I was consciously telling myself. I would eventually learn, however, that what I consciously wanted was largely insignificant.

What mattered was that I wanted my life to be lonely on a subconscious level. Therefore, I lived my life in a way that ensured this would happen and structured my life so that this invisible *purpose* would remain undiscovered. For example, I would be attracted to someone who was already committed and with whom I would have very little chance of success or, if I had a relationship, I would inevitably make excuses or create events in order for it not to develop, all on a subconscious, unaware level.

At the time, it was easy for me to blame these failures on outside circumstances of which I was a victim. However, on reflection, I could clearly see a subconscious pattern of thinking at work—with the main thought being *life is lonely*. I was thus working subconsciously to confirm this thought, to see it as a reflection of reality rather than just how my mind wanted life to be. The question then also arose: through this unconscious thinking, how much was I sabotaging myself in other areas of my life?

2
MAKING A CHOICE

*"Everything can be taken from a man but one thing:
the last of the human freedoms—to choose one's
attitude in any given circumstances, to choose
one's own way."*

— **Victor Frankl,** Man's Search for Meaning

It was on the day when the girl from the previous chapter left that I made my biggest decision—to take my life into my own hands and do whatever was required to find my bride. I started reading books, listening to podcasts, and attending seminars about life, relationships, and personal development. I quickly verified what I understood from the world of sports, namely that our beliefs about our self are a strong determining factor over our success, and that it is invaluable to have strong support (the best athletes always have so many people around them, guiding them toward success). I also knew that there were other people who had succeeded in areas where I had not, and that these people could provide clues as to the path I should take, just as I had mentored clients in tennis and given advice where possible to those who sought it.

Nevertheless, it took a lot of courage to seek help from a dear friend who could mentor me in the area I found myself lacking. This was a big step for me as, up until this point, I had not mentioned to anyone that I was unsatisfied with my dating life, and that it felt so challenging to me. Working with a mentor would mean disclosing the secrets of my insecurities that I knew how to hide so well. In hindsight, it was the best step I took, and I now regret that I didn't do this earlier in my life.

Mentorship is vital. Our mental landscape is individual to us, intangible and unique. Happiness is a challenging word to define and quantify. I realized that it was very important to find someone that could teach me how the human mind and the subconscious works in everyday life and help me clarify such well used terms as depression, awareness, happiness, mental clarity, self-belief, and imagination. I believe that if you want to succeed in a particular field then you must find someone who knows more than you do and ask for their help. It's simple, and everyone who succeeds does it. It shows strength, not weakness, to seek help from others. I guess, in a way, this is what life is all about.

With the guidance of my mentor, I eventually started asking myself some difficult questions: Why was I still single? Why did I go after girls that were engaged, married, or otherwise unattainable? Why did I feel so unattached to girls that wanted to date me? And what effect was my behavior (which I was beginning to realize was the result of these invisible thoughts that had evolved in my subconscious) having on the quality of my life?

At first, I caught myself manipulating my answers. This was because the answers to these questions were difficult for me to take. When I got a sense of what the real answers to these questions were, I was close to seeing what I was actually thinking and how I actually lived (rather than what I wanted others and myself to think), and this made me feel depressed, frightened, and even aggressive toward the outside world. Mainly this was because I couldn't see a way out, a way to change myself, after living like this for such a long time.

However, my mentor held me accountable, and encouraged me to engage truthfully with these questions. So, over time, these questions opened my eyes, as I sensed that hiding from the truth was causing me more harm than good. I noticed that my suffering could serve me, if I would be open to admitting that I was not where I wanted to be. For the first time, I realized that my loneliness was affecting my job, my reputation, and, more importantly, my self-esteem. I began to appreciate that there was no bigger obstacle to my confidence than the continuing failure to achieve my biggest goal in life—that of finding love.

My mentor taught me that while we can't control everything in our lives, we can choose how and what we think and how we interpret the events that we experience. I realized that successful people are, or learn to be, optimistic; they learn lessons from their past and use them to overcome their challenges and to become successful. This sounded so simple, but it was also confusing—hadn't I already chosen to be happily married? And, if so, what was my problem?

My mentor explained that there are two types of happiness: the visible idea of what we think will make us happy and the invisible one, which is the *purpose* our inner self wants to achieve. This purpose has unconsciously evolved over time, usually during our early years. I realized that visibly I loved the idea of having a girlfriend, as it would portray me as a successful and normal guy, but that didn't mean I wanted this invisibly or that I was ready to share my innermost vulnerabilities with a person I loved.

The mental picture I had of being in a relationship was two-dimensional and lacked the essential elements that make for a happy relationship. Up until that day, it was more important to me to maintain the self-image of appearing confident and strong, rather than being my true self—to slow down, analyze, and share with others what I was really thinking about. I began to realize how seldom, in this fast-paced life, we get the opportunity to actually do this—share with people our innermost thoughts, dreams, and fears. If we did, we would understand that there is very little difference between people, fundamentally. For the first time, I caught a glimpse of how much ungrounded fear I had in life and how this fear underpinned everything I did.

By beginning to openly share with people I trusted, I started becoming aware that I was blaming circumstances and bad luck for my loneliness. I knew that a key difference between elite athletes and the rest of the pack was that they took responsibility, rather than blaming outside forces for their results. Regrettably, this insight remained a blind spot when it concerned my personal life. My ungrounded fear of failure was stronger than the person that I (at least on a conscious level) wanted to be—someone who takes responsibility, makes decisions, and takes action.

I read a book by Victor Frankl that was recommended to me called *Man's Search for Meaning*, which describes how the author survived life in a concentration camp partly by making a choice that he would endure his suffering and find a true meaning to his existence even under such terrible circumstances. From this decision, and while surrounded by an unimaginable level of inhumanity, Frankl came to the realization that "love is the ultimate and the highest goal to which man can aspire, and the salvation of man is from love and in love."

Wow, I thought, if that man could make such choices under the horrors of a concentration camp, then I should be able to take decisions that will enable me to enjoy a fulfilled life while living in relative safety and comfort. I finally understood that to achieve this, I would need to make some serious choices and back them up with the willingness to step out of my comfort zone and take action. It was time to start engaging with who I really was and what I was really thinking, rather than sticking to mere surface changes that gave the appearance of action without really affecting anything about my life.

I acknowledged that my decision to be in a happy relationship would mean I would need to fully commit to the truth about myself, the women I was choosing, and what thoughts I had about relationships. While I knew that this kind of self-honesty would mean making difficult decisions to step outside my comfort zone, I ultimately understood that my short-term pain would serve my long-term happiness. In fact, the word decision comes from the Latin word *decider*, which means *to cut off.*

So, on that day, I decided to cut off all my excuses and make the goal of finding true love the most important task in my life, as I sincerely believed this was my missing link to happiness. Most importantly, I committed myself to continue learning from those people who could help me, who had succeeded in the areas in which I struggled, by dedicating myself to being truthful and sharing my innermost concerns.

One of my first decisions was to change the way I was searching for my future wife—rather than trying to pick up girls while completely drunk in night clubs, I decided to meet them while sober and add new social venues to my repertoire. At first, this was very difficult, and I associated quite a bit of pain and discomfort with not drinking. Suddenly, I was exposed, without the persona that I was able to put on when drunk. I felt vulnerable, not really knowing how to act or what to think. However, I knew I really wanted to meet girls that I not only found attractive but with whom I was able to genuinely connect.

Astonishingly, by presenting my real personality, free from artifice, I was able to connect with girls a lot easier and at a much deeper level. Not only was this an enjoyable and rewarding experience, I was starting to feel a lot more positive about myself and my relationships. What also helped me was to keep going back to my long-term *purpose*—contemplating the sense of joy and peace of mind I would experience from being in a happy and loving relationship.

Within less than a month, I was beginning to enjoy myself in nightclubs, free of my self-imposed inhibition and without the aid of alcohol that was so necessary before. I found this incredibly liberating. Staying sober while meeting girls helped me in so many ways: I was now able go out much more often, as I would no longer suffer from those devastating hangovers the following day; and I was able to approach girls completely sober, any time.

Thanks to this single, simple choice, I started to meet girls in a better state of mind and began to appreciate their qualities beyond simply the way they looked. It is worth remembering that, at first, I found talking to women I liked a difficult and cringe-worthy experience. However, by learning from these rather embarrassing events, using the tools that I was taught during this time (the tools that I will share with you later in this book and on video), and maintaining the discipline to keep working consistently on my self-development and not give up, it was a great surprise to me how quickly it became easy to connect with potential partners.

3

THE BIGGEST LESSONS OF LIFE

"Insanity: doing the same thing over and over again and expecting a different result."

— **Albert Einstein**

Ever since I read Neil Strauss's book, *The Game*, I thought I understood that dating skills included the ability to attract girls as well as bonding with them. A key proposal in his book was that to attract a partner, one needed to be fun and interesting. I noticed how many dates became boring as a result of standardized interview-type questions, and I quickly learned that I would need to lead more entertaining and inspiring conversations to make dates last.

I also worked on my looks, went to the gym, read books on the laws of attraction, and made sure my dates would be a lot of fun. However, my subconscious—or unaware—thinking pattern of avoiding girls that liked me, while obsessing about the ones that were unattainable, continued. I was only scraping the surface of what was really holding me back. Rather than examining and ending the thoughts that were stopping my freedom of expression, I was seeking quick fixes. My inner thermostat was still set for remaining single.

Although I was making some progress, and more and more women seemed to be in my life, I was still essentially a single man that had no luck with women at all. I was more focused on collecting phone numbers and dates than actually finding love. When a girl liked me, I would tell myself that I could do better, and compare her with the other girls I knew. This was then a perfect reason to break off the relationship. And when a girl didn't like me, I started obsessing about her, thinking she would be the woman of my dreams. This behavior was the perfect way to experience dating as something extremely frustrating. The result usually was that I would end up dating no one.

The real reason I was not progressing was that I was doing the same things over and over again, but on an invisible level. Through teachings from The Kogan Academy, I was beginning to understand that our minds have the capacity to generalize our experiences unbeknownst to our conscious self. Our minds create *common denominators* or important generalized thoughts that have evolved from such influences as our relationships with our parents or main caregivers, the key events in our childhoods, our first sexual experiences, our earliest memories, and so on.

As we develop from our childhood, so does our invisible/subconscious thinking, and these thoughts begin to think themselves, irrespective of circumstances. They're usually perceived as impressions or pictures in our mind's eye, and these usually unobserved thoughts have the biggest influence on our perceptions of reality. For example, I lost count of how many times, when I saw a car driven poorly, without seeing the driver, I would automatically assume it was driven by a woman—an indication that I had an invisible, generalized thought along the lines of "women are stupid." I was thus beginning to realize that, before anything, it was important to identify the correct names of these impressions in my head, and find out how and why they were there before I could make any change in my love life.

Until we learn to see our own thinking, and observe and understand how this thinking affects our lives, and until we then learn how to end these patterns of thinking so that they no longer influence our lives, it will be almost impossible to experience real breakthroughs in key areas. In a way, our thoughts work in the same manner as electricity. We know electricity is there and we can see its effects, but it remains invisible to us. Our world depends on electricity to run properly while, and it can cause catastrophic problems if mistreated or neglected.

In dating, I was committed only to the visible aspects or thoughts, including things like looks and wealth, which can affect attraction, as well as conversation and dating skills that might affect bonding. These have some degree of importance. However, the invisible aspects of our minds, the ones that are usually unobserved in our busy, fast-paced lives—our thoughts, beliefs, and feelings—are what really determine our dating success. Without addressing them, any other change remains cosmetic, meaning that my results would stay the same.

A good analogy that helped me grasp this concept is that of a fruit tree. The fruits represent results, which are what most people look at. We either like them or would prefer to change them. But it is what grows under the surface that creates the fruits, namely the seeds and the roots, and these are usually invisible and therefore unobserved. This sounds so clear, but it took me some time to really grasp. Once I did understand this, I became a different person. I finally realized that if I wanted to change the 'fruits,' I would first have to change the 'roots.' The fruits are the current thoughts that are visible to us, while the seeds and roots are our thinking, and what is really going on inside our head.

Many people wish to be in a fulfilling relationship, but they fail because they don't have the inner capacity to expose themselves to the beauty of true love and intimacy. The root of this problem lies with their beliefs about themselves, relationships, sex, and men or women in general. Only by changing these beliefs can we change our results.

I learned that as long as I was unaware of the existence of these invisible thought patterns, I would be unable to change the results I was getting with regard to my dating life. I would meet so many different women, and yet I was unable to turn any of those liaisons into a lasting relationship, as my inner thermostat was set to keep me single. In hindsight, before discovering The Kogan Academy, I remember that speaking openly about intimate topics made me cringe, which was a clear indication that I had some limiting thoughts about sex. I could do whatever I wanted but, as long as I was simply trying to change the fruits, without addressing the roots, the outcome stayed the same.

4
MENTAL LAWS TO SUCCESS

"The man of action has the present, but the thinker controls the future."

— **Oliver Wendell Holmes**

I came to understand a fundamental truth: our success or failure in any and every aspect of life depends on what goes on inside our heads, period. Every facet of our lives, every decision we have made, how we look, how we sound, what we eat, our beliefs, our opinions, the people we attract, every nuance of our personality all depend on what we think and the quality of our thinking. In fact, it was the famous Greek philosopher, Socrates, who was the first to claim that there are rules of nature, including mental laws, and that we can choose whether or not we live in harmony with them. Therefore, I started reading many books on thinking and learned some basic mental laws, which I would like to share with you.

Best-selling author Brian Tracy speaks about seven mental laws to success, a few of which I would like to mention here. A key mental law is the *law of control*. This states that we are happy to the degree that we feel we are in control of the outcomes of our lives. For a very long time, I left my dating life to chance, hoping that one day I would enjoy the kind of relationship I was so desperately seeking. Of course, by doing so, I was giving myself no control over this important aspect of my life. However, once I decided to take my dating life into my own hands, I instantly felt that I was able to influence the quality of my life. I started creating clarity about what I wanted, why I wasn't getting there, and what I needed to do to progress.

A related mental law is the *law of cause and effect*, which states that we are the results of all the actions we take, and that our actions are the results of our thoughts. This law taught me that my past actions had caused me to remain single, and that they would continue to do so unless I made some changes. As mentioned earlier, I had realized that I had some strong patterns of thinking that kept me away from developing deeper personal relationships.

Identifying these causes felt very empowering, as it gave me a sense that I was more in control of my life. I had started to take more responsibility over my life and its outcomes. The most important application of this *law of control* is that our thoughts are the causes of our actions and condition the effects of our lives. This law explains that whatever we dwell upon grows and expands in our lives. This is the reason why we must create the thoughts that support our quest to be in a fulfilling relationship. This knowledge can be applied to improving any facet of your life.

This law sounds like quite a daring statement but, if you think about it for a moment, does it not often happen in our daily life that we come across what we're thinking about? For example, I recall the time when I wanted to buy a new black Jeep, and I was suddenly seeing exactly that car wherever I went. In a similar way, I experienced an abundance of girls I was attracted to once I really started looking out for 'serious' dates. In fact, our brain even has a part called the reticular activating system (RAS), which is responsible for regulating arousal and which helps us to notice the things we're focused on. It operates as a filter between our conscious mind and our subconscious mind, by taking instructions from the former and passing them on to the latter. By analyzing millions of bytes of information per second, the RAS then subconsciously filters out irrelevant information and allows us to focus on what we want, without getting overwhelmed.

Maybe the most critical mental law I learned is the *law of correspondence*: it states that our outer world is a mirror of what is going on in our mind, meaning we become what we think about most of the time. The law of correspondence and the *law of attraction* work hand in hand, as they explain how we attract a person with similar thoughts and beliefs to our own, and how we repulse people and circumstances that contradict our most dominant thoughts.

What all the mental laws have in common is that they state that any thought or idea held continuously in the conscious mind will become reality. Therefore, we can reset the inner thermostat that's keeping us within our comfort zone simply by changing the way we think.

5
THE SCIENCE OF ACTING

"The destiny of every human being is dictated by what goes on inside his skull when he is confronted with what goes on outside his skull."

— **Eric Berne**

My mentor was learning to become an actor at a drama conservatoire called The Kogan Academy of Dramatic Arts, which teaches a standalone acting theory called the science of acting, developed by the academy's founder Sam Kogan. The science of acting is the body of knowledge created and developed from the academy since its inception in 1991.

The science of acting evolved from the concept that a deeper understanding of one's self creates a deeper understanding of the character the actor is playing and therefore a far greater quality of performance. This body of knowledge includes a full study of the human mind and explains the subconscious and how it affects our behavior and lives in clear and simple terms.

Students learn how to think just the thoughts of the character, free from any of their own patterns of thinking and free from any thoughts of being observed —thus creating a performance of the highest quality. To become a good actor, *The Science of Acting* teaches that it is essential to develop self-awareness; that is, to become aware of thinking that may have been unobserved until now and which may be an obstacle to the creative process. What students essentially learn is how thinking works, so that they can develop an agile mindset that allows them to choose to adopt the thinking that is most conducive to a great performance. It is clear that this knowledge has amazing potential in all areas of life.

When my mentor told me about this theory, I became extremely curious. Unless they're aware of their thinking and why they think the way they do, most people have a rigid consciousness, which is one of the reasons why people suffer from stress and depression, make the same mistakes over and over again, and seldom change. Their fixed attitude predetermines their responses and their interpretations of life situations. I instantly sensed how the science of acting could be applied to so many areas including sports, business, conflict resolution, and possibly relationships. What I didn't realize was that by learning more about the science of acting, I was going to transform my personal life.

The school offered me lessons in their theory, which closely analyzes a person's thinking. By taking their classes, I literally transformed my life. I can easily say that this was one of the best things I have ever started, and remains so to this day. Like a muscle, I realized that our mind is something we can train, the big difference being that it is by far our most important muscle in terms of fulfilling our potential. In fact, science has discovered that our brain continuously changes by creating new neural pathways, which is absolutely amazing. And, to me, the science of acting not only explains the way our mind works better than anything else I have ever encountered, but it also provides effective tools that have enabled me to experience fulfilling relationships.

In the next few chapters, I will explain in very general terms a few key concepts that have affected my life. For a deeper understanding and introduction to this topic, please visit allonkhakhsouri.com/free.

6
How We Learn

"Many people would rather die than think.
In fact, they do."

— Bertrand Russell

The theory of the science of acting explains that we have reference points, which are innate. For example, wanting to have a fulfilled life, to procreate, and to belong to a group are among some of those natural reference points. They also include the inborn ability and drive to be in an intimate relationship. At the same time, we also adopt acquired reference points from exploring the world and being influenced by key people in our lives, such as our parents. These acquired reference points are the result of what the psychologist Ivan Pavlov called *conditioning*.

Pavlov became famous for an experiment he tried of continuously ringing a bell before feeding some dogs. He found that after some time, the dogs would salivate to the sound of the bell itself, even when no food was present. They had created a link between the bell and food. Pavlov explained how animals and people create conditioned behaviors which, over time, become unaware, invisible, and automatic.

This experiment showed how each thought activates other thoughts. The science of acting theory calls this circle of thoughts *complexes*; when one thought is activated, then so are the others to different degrees. Similarly, our thoughts about topics such as the opposite sex or dating will naturally activate further thoughts which, in turn, activate still more thoughts. As complexes work automatically, we can't stop them without becoming aware of them. This is how they run our life. At the same time, they enable us to learn.

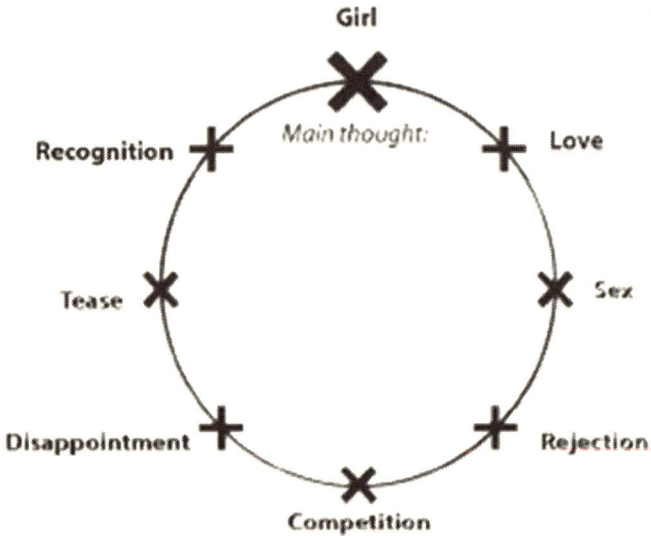

Figure 1: The big X is the main thought which, when activated, also activates all the other ones to different degrees (adapted from Sam Kogan, The Science of Acting).

Unfortunately, some complexes harm us. For example, I was raised in a culture where people didn't express their emotions openly, nor did they speak much about sexual topics. Therefore, I acquired the reference points that it was common not to reveal my emotions toward other people, including girls I liked. Rather, I would hide my true intentions, while at the same time hoping that girls would take the initiative. By depriving myself of the ability to express myself and my natural drive, I turned potential girlfriends into buddies. This felt extremely frustrating and created strong negative associations to dating.

Of course, I desperately wanted to change this, but I didn't know how. One way I coped with this on a more subconscious level was to avoid dates or to make them go sour as quickly as possible. I remember one incident where I bumped into a girl I found extremely attractive. I saw her sitting having a coffee with another friend, and she instantly waved me over.

As we spoke, I noticed she really seemed to like me, and I felt she was indicating that she wanted me to ask her out. Strange as this sounds, this caused me to experience a flush of thoughts that made me feel very anxious. There I was, with no cover, standing in front of the girl I adored, and who was giving me all the signals that she felt the same. I was blushing like crazy. I became completely red and sweaty, and felt very uncomfortable. In that moment, I wanted to disappear. So, I took the first opportunity to tell her I had to go, and I rushed away. I completely blew the opportunity and sabotaged myself.

I can see now how the interaction with this girl triggered my more visible thoughts like: "I'm making a fool out of myself," "What if she finds out I'm not as cool as I act?" and "What if she's just teasing me?" These ungrounded, visible thoughts were, of course, part of a greater invisible complex of thoughts that I was not aware of at the time.

Within this complex were thoughts regarding what I wanted to achieve at the time (I wanted to be rejected), and about what I generally thought about myself (I'm inferior), about women (women are frightening), about relationships (relationships are not for me), about life (life is lonely), about sex (I'll leave that one to your imagination, dear reader), and so on. The outcome of this event only served to strengthen and confirm these invisible thoughts and thus my conscious and visible beliefs. Altogether, they made me want to fail in my dating life, as I feared these moments of embarrassment and felt safest on my own—failing was the least stressful option.

It took me some time to see and then to learn how to properly change these thought processes, but it is possible when you know how. The key is to learn to reflect, watch, and find out what goes on in our head free from any stress of wanting results. Thanks to *The Science of Acting*, I was able to create new complexes that helped me form a loving and healthy relationship with my wife, while dismantling the ones that were harmful to this cause.

7
PAIN AND PLEASURE

"The secret of success is learning how to use pain and pleasure instead of having pain and pleasure use you. If you do that, you're in control of your life. If you don't, life controls you."

— Anthony Robbins

Leadership guru and self-help expert Anthony Robbins uses a different way to explain these associations between different thoughts. He says that we human beings are all driven by the desire for pleasure and the need to avoid pain. As human beings are not random creatures, all of our thought processes really serve to help us survive. Therefore, it would seem that our thoughts should promote happy relationships, a family, and children—after all, this seems to be our natural predisposition.

Robbins suggests that what complicates matters is that certain experiences will promote a specific feeling and can often create a mismatch between the actual trigger of that feeling and its perceived cause. This mismatch will usually be invisible and serve to make us either avoid similar experiences in the future, if they are perceived as painful; or seek them out, if they are perceived as pleasurable. He uses the example of a small kid to illustrate how these mismatches can happen: when an infant crawls on a bed he has no idea that falling off can cause pain. So, when he does fall off the bed, he's not fully aware what caused the pain and, if it happens again, his brain might attach the feeling of pain to the bed, hence creating a fear of beds!

These mismatches are responsible for seemingly bizarre and invisible desires such as wanting to remain single, as childhood experiences may form complexes that attach a lot of pain to experiences with the opposite sex. For instance, I remember that as a youngster, I was called "ugly" on a few occasions and, although I may have matured into a good-looking guy, I had formed a complex about myself being unattractive. I thought this about myself irrespective of how I actually looked or was perceived.

Sadly, I believe this ungrounded invisible thought is very common among people. The problem was that by thinking this thought frequently and unknowingly, it had a negative effect on my general state of mind, my self-confidence, and my appearance. By thinking this thought, I was achieving it, strengthening it, and confirming it to myself as a reflection of reality—it was a self-sabotaging downward spiral. This affected the way I interacted with women. In order to avoid painful feelings of rejection and failure, I developed a behavior of wanting to continually appease and impress them.

While these covers served to protect me, they also created a serious barrier toward creating intimate relationships. Trying to act like a superhero all the time was extremely tiring and created another complex that linked lots of stress to girls. To make things worse, my relief from these stresses was through drinking, which formed yet another complex, linking pleasure to being around women while drinking and partying. This is why I enjoyed putting lots of energy into nightlife. Together, these complexes ensured that I would stay away from committed relationships. In a way, I had unconsciously decided that relationships were not for me.

8
VISIBLE AND INVISIBLE THOUGHTS

"We don't see things as they are; we see them as we are."

— Anais Nin

Up until I began to study *The Science of Acting*, I was blissfully unaware. Although 'blissful' is perhaps not the right word in this case; as I have explained, certain invisible patterns of thinking were causing me a great deal of suffering. This prompted a question in my mind: why is so much of our thinking (the thinking that underpins most of our behavior, and determines our choices, our happiness, and our lives) invisible to us, and why are our unconscious desires so often the exact opposite of what we think we visibly want? I never understood how invisible thoughts were running my life. This is why it became so frustrating that I was not making progress in my dating life.

Ultimately, life would be very difficult if we experienced and remembered all our thoughts consciously, as it would become very hard to place our focus on a specific topic. Invisible thoughts thus serve two main functions: firstly, they create automated processes whereby we can master activities without thinking of them at all. This allows us to focus on new challenges. The more we learn, the more thoughts are added to each complex, until eventually the complexes themselves become part of other, bigger complexes.

An example of this can be seen from the process of learning to drive a car: initially, it takes quite a lot of conscious effort to control the car but, over time, we drive effortlessly and involuntarily. Driving becomes an unconscious motor effort, part of our repertoire of unconscious responses. It is logical that all of our complexes work in the same way, once they have been formed. They think themselves, irrespective of the circumstances we're in.

Secondly, at some point in our lives we've made a decision that we prefer not to actively see certain thoughts. This is because they seem so frightening to us that we think that if we become fully aware of them, they will prevent us from functioning efficiently. For example, a child may have a thought that they blame themselves for their mother's unhappiness or anger, and fear that she may not want them. This is a very frightening thought for a child. As children, we know life would be very difficult without a parent's love and care so, in order to get rid of the fear of this thought, the child may suppress it. Being a child, they cannot think such a frightening thought through rationally until the fear depletes in the same way an adult can. The thought remains unfinished, and such thoughts can affect their actions and their other thoughts, creating patterns of thinking that have a great influence on the rest of their life.

9
Fear And Shame

"A warrior accepts that we can never know what will happen to us next. We can try to control the uncontrollable by looking for security and predictability, always hoping to be comfortable and safe. But the truth is that we can never avoid uncertainty. This not-knowing is part of the adventure. It's also what makes us afraid."

— Pema Chodron

For most of us, there is nothing scarier than seeing a beautiful person in the middle of the day and thinking about approaching them. I can't remember how often I missed out on such opportunities to chat with women that could have ended up being perfect girlfriends. Yet, at the same time, I also recall that when I did drum up some courage, girls would usually respond very positively. So, why do so many of us suffer from such fear?

It is mainly a direct result of the early experiences in our lives with the opposite sex, going right back to the first person in our lives who took care of us, and the generalized and unfinished thoughts that have evolved as a result of these experiences.

As kids, our minds are malleable and outside influences mold us. In our early years, we strive to get our emotional needs met by our parents, while during our teens we long to be accepted and appreciated by our peers. We all crave to be loved and respected while, at the same time, we fear to be abandoned or ridiculed.

The Kogan Academy of Dramatic Arts uses a play by Nikolai Gogol called *Marriage* as an example to explain how early memories of fear can run our lives. The main character of the story is called Podkolyosin. He's a bachelor that hires a matchmaker to find himself a wife. In the final scene however, he runs away from the woman he is about to get married to. Throughout the book, it becomes apparent that although our main character is supposedly seeking a wife, he never intended to marry.

An interpretation for this traces Podkolyosin's resistance to a childhood experience, where the small boy overheard his mother scream out loud while making love to his father. Although he heard screams of pleasure, the boy thought his father was hurting his beloved mother, and formed a complex that men hurt women while having sex and that sex was abuse. This incident gave rise to invisible thoughts such as *sex is frightening*, *women are not for me*, and *sex is not for me*. Podkolyosin chose to think these thoughts—to be faithful to his mother—which stopped him from marrying. Of course, another person would have responded differently, but the story nevertheless illustrates very well how invisible thoughts can run our lives.

Similar to fear, feelings of shame create a serious obstacle to forming healthy relationships with other people. When young, we often don't have the emotional intelligence, experience, or support to grieve over painful events, so these thoughts and emotions have been repressed. This can include simple moments like not getting the full attention of the people who are in our charge or, on the other end of the scale, receiving too much attention from a needy parent. The imprints of such experiences remain in our minds and become stronger with each new shameful incident so that, eventually, they become an important influence on our development as a person.

Both fear and shame create strong imprints in our consciousness that consist of invisible thoughts that think themselves irrespective of circumstance. They make us see ourselves, other people, and the world through extremely subjective lenses, without even being aware that we're seeing things in a biased way. These lasting feelings are often the results of not making sense of events we've experienced. As a result, people often feel either completely inadequate and act very timid and shy, or they try to overplay insecurities by playing the character of the super confident and cool persona. Either way, feelings of fear and shame cause many of us to feel uncomfortable in our own skin, at least on an invisible level.

Such thoughts are unpleasant, which is why we suppress them. Many of us tend to escape feelings of pain and discomfort by losing ourselves through some external means, such as work, TV, fantasies, or other forms of addictive behavior. I remember being fourteen years old and wanting to impress my friends by showing myself to be an 'experienced' drinker. That night, we were hanging out at a friend's house, and I ended up drinking various beverages from his parents' alcohol cabinet. The next morning I woke up with women dressed in white telling me that I was in a hospital, as I had alcohol poisoning.

Although I never had a serious drinking problem, it did become a habit of mine to get completely wasted at nightclubs and then play my role as the womanizer. Nightlife was one way of losing myself from my internalized feelings of fear and shame. With the great benefit of hindsight, I can see now how much I thought that "I had no life."

At the time, this felt like a true reflection of reality and thus why I needed to lose myself from it so much. However, I only perceived my life this way because I had a strong invisible thought that "I have no life." Back then, if someone would have told me this, I would probably have laughed in their face, strongly denied it, and gone back to the nightclub. At the time, this invisible thought was very shameful, and I certainly didn't want to be discovered as having it.

In fact, my life was lived in a way to ensure that this thought was hidden from myself and the world. The thought, "I have no life," was also the root cause of me wanting to be on my own; I needed to engage with this thought, understand why it was there, and finish it off before I could develop a relationship that was anything other than superficial. It's an important step to also look at your own stories that you're telling yourself. What is the root cause of you currently being on your own? It isn't an easy question to ask yourself or answer, but it is important to consider. (If you need assistance on getting to the foundation of your beliefs, I have worked with many people professionally and personally over the years.

You can visit
www.allonkhakshouri.com/free/
or
email info@scienceofacting.com.

Ironically, these games may have been an influence on me becoming the agent of three world number-one tennis players. However, I was also losing myself in this fantasy world to avoid the complex of the thought "I have no life." I had thoughts about myself like "I'm incapable" and "I'm inferior." As a byproduct of frequently wanting to impress someone, losing myself in nightclubs, and playing games in my head, these invisible thoughts were becoming stronger—my ditch was getting deeper, and I was getting further and further away from what I dreamed of achieving. And it all stemmed from one simple invisible thought.

Research has shown that when we repress thoughts, especially those that invoke strong feelings, they become stronger (invisibly, of course). It's like telling yourself not to think of a pink elephant—just the suggestion will make you think of it. The reason this is so, is that our sub consciousness monitors our desire to stop thinking about the pink elephant, and ends up focusing on exactly that, unless we place our conscious thoughts onto something else.

When we suppress unwanted, shameful thoughts and replace them with other, more socially acceptable thoughts (i.e. replacing the thought that *I'm inferior* or *I don't know how to think* with the thought *I'm superior* or the purpose of *impressing people*) we end up making the suppressed thought stronger. Furthermore, the more frequently we think the visible suppressant thought (*I'm strong*), the stronger and more influential the suppressed thought (*I'm weak*) becomes in our lives.

10
AWARENESS AND
SELF-CONDITIONING

*"What is necessary to change a person is to
change his awareness of himself."*

— **Abraham**

I have briefly looked at how our subconscious or invisible thoughts can run our lives without us realizing. They make us do things without knowing why. A good example is continuing to smoke cigarettes, when there is solid evidence that doing so can drastically shorten our lives. Staying single is, of course, another. This is why it is essential to become aware of our invisible thoughts and the sensations that are boiling under our skin. Only by placing our attention on our inner world can we break the patterns of habit. By being engaged with our thoughts and feelings, we can work on making sense of how they've been formed. Therefore, awareness of ourselves and our thought processes is really the key to changing our lives.

Engagement here means having the ability to see and analyze our own thinking, so that we can then choose the thoughts and feelings we would like to have. Once we become aware of our own thoughts and feelings, it becomes possible for us to also become aware of the thoughts and feelings of others. This becomes very connecting, as all people long to be understood. However, without such awareness, self-conditioning happens automatically, as our brain economizes on the use of our attention. The worst form of such self-conditioning is learned helplessness.

A good example of how this happens can be seen from a baby elephant that is tied to a bamboo tree. In the beginning, the elephant tries to resist with all its force, until it realizes that it is unable to escape. After repeating this ritual for a few days, the elephant no longer tries. So, years later, the fully grown elephant can still be tied to a small bamboo stick and won't try to break free, despite the fact that it could easily do so. This is because the elephant has taught itself to be helpless and no longer even desires to challenge this idea. This mental submission can also be seen in humans.

When we are young, we are malleable; our minds are vulnerable to conditioning. For example, when a teacher tells us we're not good at math, we start to believe this and, as I'm sure you understand, if we think we aren't good at something, there is little chance that we ever will be. If we have thoughts like this frequently, they can form an invisible purpose that we subconsciously want to achieve—labeled, for instance, "I want to fail" or "I want to be helpless." In the same way, a few unpleasant experiences with the opposite sex may cause us to believe that relationships are simply not for us. In both cases, we teach ourselves to be helpless and no longer see things as they really are.

I remember having experienced a few embarrassing moments with girls as a kid, like being ridiculed in front of all my friends when I told a girl I liked her. These early events, with their long-lasting feelings of discomfort, made me very fearful to approach women, especially in daytime settings where other people could see my attempts. Of course, I repressed these feelings by finding socially acceptable excuses like, "She probably has a boyfriend," "She's probably boring," and "I didn't really like her anyway." By repressing my fears, I strengthened my anxieties and gradually conditioned myself to *learned helplessness with regard to dating*. In fact, I remember that even when dates would go well, I'd try and think of ways not to mess them up. By doing so, I was indirectly anticipating things not going well, and I provoked myself to choke and make my fears of failure come true.

Luckily, our consciousness is not set in stone. By noticing that we often act unconsciously, and by becoming aware of our feelings and thoughts, we can also appreciate how they are no longer relevant to our current life. This is why learning to catch my invisible thoughts, even for trivial matters, has been very valuable to me. Thanks to this skill, I've become more aware of my thinking and, as a result, happier, while training myself to develop a more agile mind. Once we learn to catch our invisible thoughts, we create a choice in our life to live a meaningful life and fulfill our dreams.

11
Chamber Of
Visible Thinking

*"The ultimate value of life depends upon
awareness and the power of contemplation
rather than mere survival."*

— **Aristotle**

Thanks to the Model of Awareness, which they teach at The Kogan Academy, I now have a better picture of how thinking works and how to become more aware. I will try to explain.

Let's imagine a box with a line going horizontally across it close to the top. The smaller space above this line is called the Chamber of Visible Thinking (CVT). Visible thoughts are all the thoughts that can be seen within the CVT, the thoughts that we're aware of. They are conscious commands that we can control. For example, if I asked you to think of your house, you should pretty much straight away see a picture of the house that has been stored in your mind.

Below the CVT we have the larger area of the box consisting of thoughts that are currently unobserved, but which are observable if we know how to look correctly. These thoughts remain invisible to us until we make ourselves aware of them and can see the complexes that are attached to them. There are some thoughts within this model that will always remain invisible, as there seems no purpose for us to see them —such as the ones that regulate biological functions.

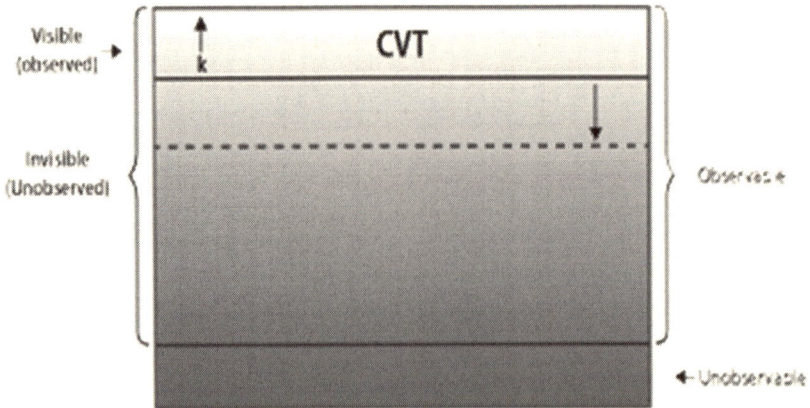

Figure 2: *The Model of Awareness (Adapted from Sam Kogan, The Science of Acting).*

When we engage with our thoughts, we are simply lowering the line of the CVT at will, so that we can see our patterns of thinking. The more questions we ask ourselves, the easier it will be. We start understanding why we think the way we do in order to change it, if necessary, for the better. Our goal is to become aware of our observable yet unobserved thoughts, by stretching our CVT and our awareness. These thoughts have been stuck in the invisible section of our mind because, at some point in our lives, we made a decision that we did not want to see them, in many cases because they generated so much fear and shame. Every time we think similar thoughts, whether visibly or invisibly, they join with all of our other thoughts of the same kind from across the years.

For example, each time I used to encounter attractive girls, I would visibly want to impress them. This is the way I lived. By the time I was meeting and talking with lots of attractive girls in my life, I had unknowingly learned how to successfully cover up my real thoughts and get through my life by keeping shameful thoughts like "I have no life," "I'm incapable," or "I'm inferior" undiscovered.

Again, you must understand that, at the time, I had no idea I was thinking these thoughts at all. If you had asked me if I was happy back then, I would probably have said yes. In fact, I would probably have done anything to avoid really answering this question sincerely.

To me, life was the hand that I was dealt. It had nothing to do with what I subconsciously thought. As a result of wanting to impress and of pretending that I could achieve anything I wanted, I was also strengthening the respective complexes related to the invisible thoughts, as well as other related thoughts I may have had about myself, women, and life in general. Together, they would influence my general thinking, my goals (of wanting to stay single and undiscovered) and, as a result, my life.

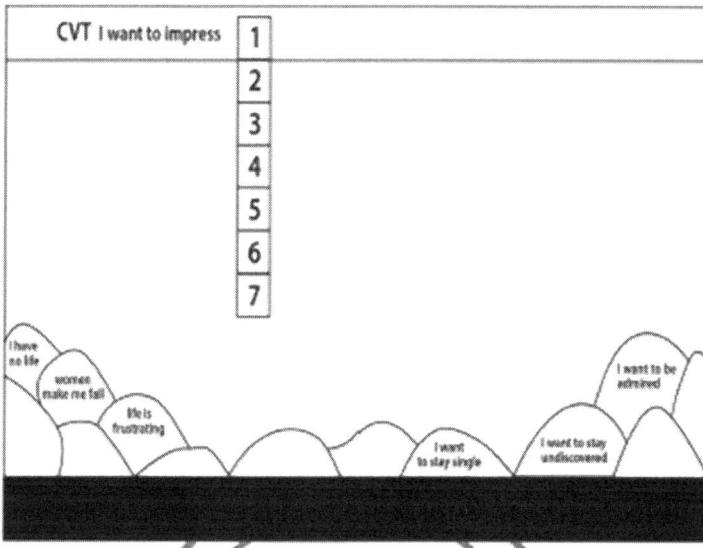

Figure 3: *The Model of Awareness demonstrates how each invisible thought forms a res, which grows over the years every time a similar idea is thought. These residues form complexes that become stronger and stronger each time the related ideas are thought. This increases the influence that these thoughts have on a person's life (adapted from Sam Kogan, The Science of Acting).*

By looking at the thoughts that have caused our CVT to shrink, we can appreciate that everyone has these kind of thoughts, and see them for what they are—just thoughts. By increasing our awareness, we allow ourselves to make sense of the thought patterns that have run our lives, and thereby take a first step to reprogramming ourselves in the areas we would like to, by preventing past feelings of fear and shame from running our lives. This will be a key goal in the second part of the book.

12
The Philosophy Of Growth

"Love is the will to extend oneself for the purpose of nurturing one's own or another's spiritual growth."

— M. Scott Peck

By developing an agile consciousness, I realized that our life does not need to be directed by fear and shame, and that we have the power to grow and change. John W. Atkinson ran a study that involved groups of children in reward-based games. The kids that enjoyed high achievement focused on the reward of achieving the task, while those with low achievement were driven by the fear and humiliation of failure. Their fears resulted in them either avoiding the challenge altogether, or attempting it in a way that made it almost impossible to succeed.

Atkinson introduced a game of throwing hoops onto a peg, in which the ones with high achievement motivation stood a bold but still realistic distance from the peg, while those driven by fear of failure often stood very closely to the peg, as they did not believe they could master this challenge from a distance. Interestingly though, many fear-driven candidates also stood so far back that it was impossible for them to be successful. He concluded they did this to avoid any shame when they inevitably failed.

Bernard Weiner published his attribution theory, in which he noted that having a positive frame of mind is based on an 'internal locus of control,' which results in a self-belief that we can control or respond to external factors. In contrast, a negative frame of mind is based on an 'external locus of control,' meaning we do not feel we are in control of our destiny.

Carol S. Dweck makes a similar point in her excellent book *Mindset*. She argues that personality and skills are not a fixed trait but rather something we can develop. She distinguishes between a 'growth mindset' and a 'fixed mindset' and explains the differences between these two groups—people with a fixed mindset have a propensity to allow their fears and feelings of shame to give them the impression that they're always being judged and labeled, so they must continuously defend themselves to enjoy appreciation and validation.

They also tend to judge and label others, as all their validation depends on outside factors. Their rigid consciousness promotes unfinished thinking, which makes change very hard. In contrast, people with a growth mindset are willing to take risks and exert effort to learn and change. They pick up accurate information about their current abilities and are able to develop the awareness to identify their own strengths and weaknesses. As a result of their more agile mind, they can convert setbacks into future successes. By believing in their 'internal locus of control,' they continuously develop as human beings.

Dweck explains how children are all born with a drive to learn but, once they reach an age at which they can evaluate themselves, some become scared and teach themselves to be helpless and fail, as they fear big challenges. She uses many examples to demonstrate the difference between children with a fixed mindset and those with a growth mindset.

For instance, she asked four-year-old kids to solve jigsaw puzzles and, after a while, offered them harder puzzles. The kids with a fixed mindset would want to play it safe and continue using the same puzzles, while those with the growth mindset immediately took on the new challenge.

In another piece of research, kids with both mindsets were given some easy riddles. Both groups solved them very well. Then they were given unsolvable riddles. Those with the fixed mindsets gave up much quicker than those with a growth mindset, who didn't seem to want to give up. In a final test, all the kids were given easy challenges again. The interesting finding was that, again, the kids with the growth mindset solved the quizzes very easily, while those with a fixed mindset struggled. Some even refused to try them, fearing that they could embarrass themselves, as they felt they had done with the more difficult puzzles. They had taught themselves learned helplessness.

I remember being afraid of embarrassing myself in front of others, and therefore trying to compensate for my insecurities by trying to continuously prove myself as being better. Setbacks would make me feel devastated, which is why I would often avoid new challenges, including the one of finding lasting love. Instead, I chose to enjoy a secure and predictable life and kept my invisible thoughts undiscovered by myself and other people. By doing so, of course, I made myself fail in possibly the most crucial part of my life.

Luckily, I was able to change my destiny. Through a journey in personal development, I have learned that the key to real success is a commitment to learning and growing. I found that this kind of 'growth mindset' has been even more critical in creating intimate relationships, as the topic of love involves thoughts about myself, my partner, and relationships in general. I also discovered that being curious, and seeking novelty and challenges, not only feels fulfilling, but also makes a person more attractive towards members of the opposite sex.

By seeing these three aspects of relationships with an agile mindset, I learned to appreciate that we're all evolving as human beings, and that love is about nurturing the spiritual growth of both our loved ones and ourselves. I accepted that we're born as near perfect beings, all equal to each other; but, because of our individual and unique experiences and the thinking that develops as a result, we often mess ourselves up. This is why I believe that by developing an agile consciousness with a growth mindset, anybody can create a purpose of wanting to be in a fulfilling relationship.

13
PURPOSES

"There are no evil, angry, or aggressive people, only unhappy people in pursuit of their happiness."

— **Yevgeny Vakhtangov,** Russian director

As humans, we always want something more or better. This is the engine of evolution and progress. Whether we want to find a partner, stay alone, be loved, or be rejected these are all wants or *purposes*. A purpose is a change we want to achieve, because we think it will make us happy.

The Science of Acting explains how such purposes are formed, and uses the following metaphor to explain: picture a man who regularly walks across a field. The more he walks across the same route, the easier it becomes, as his steps form a path which is comfortable to walk on. In this metaphor, we are the man, the field is our consciousness, and the path is a purpose. Now imagine that we walk the same path so often that it becomes deeper and deeper, until eventually it is a ditch from which we can no longer climb out. In life, we call this land erosion. However, we are now in what the Kogan Academy calls a 'mind erosion.'

Figure 4: Man walking on a field.

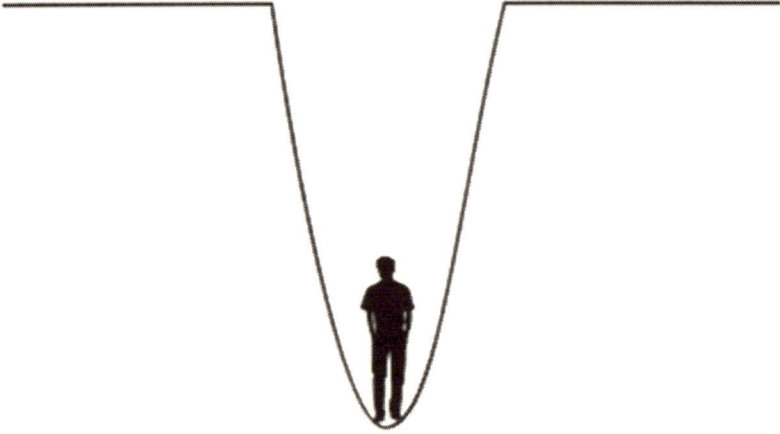

Figure 5: The man is so deep in his ditch he can't see out. This is the equivalent of a 'mind erosion' (both adapted from Sam Kogan, The Science of Acting).

Mind erosions are formed in our heads by thinking the same thoughts over and over again. We do this regardless of whether we're aware of it or not, by creating patterns of thinking which we follow irrespective of visible circumstances. Eventually, they become like deep ditches in a field, which we are unable to climb out of or see any alternative to. The more we get used to our purpose, the more normal it feels, so it becomes very hard to choose a different one. This is an unaware mental process; the purposes that run our lives are invisible to a greater or lesser degree, depending on the individual; that is unless we learn or are taught to see them.

Internalized feelings of fear and shame can deprive us of the ability to enjoy our lives and freely express ourselves, and they can prevent us from achieving our innermost goals. They often shut down some of our most basic needs. This is why it can become easy to derail from our fundamental purposes, such as wanting to be in a happy relationship. This purpose seems to be a significant element to fulfillment in life. In my case, my mind erosion was related to thoughts of feeling safest when being single, as the many inadequacies I believed I had would remain undiscovered. Of course, I knew that people expected me to get married and have kids and visibly I wanted this for myself as well.

Of course, it was painful and even embarrassing to me that I was not able to find a partner and sustain a lasting relationship. To lose myself from this shame, I would spend time getting drunk at parties, and hiding behind the cover of enjoying my single life. My belief was that by looking like someone who didn't want to be in a relationship, nobody would suspect me of having limiting beliefs that were preventing me from achieving my innermost desires. This is how I covered up my shame with what I believed to be more socially acceptable behavior. Unfortunately, by playing this role, I also strengthened my purpose of wanting to be single.

Through *The Science of Acting,* I learned that I would need to change my purposes to achieve different results in my life. The way I did this was by filling my head with lots of pictures and sense data of being in a fulfilling relationship, and associating those thoughts with lots of joy. My goal was to get my consciousness comfortable with the very thoughts that made me cringe. For example, I would imagine sharing very intimate and personal stories with my partner and feeling not only accepted and loved, but also allowing her to open up to me.

The Science of Acting speaks about purposes in great detail, as they are crucial to the way we conduct our life. What is important here is that in order to be happy, we need to create an agile consciousness that allows us to choose our purposes at will, including the purpose of being in a fulfilled intimate relationship. We will come back in Part Two of the book to this important topic.

14
RESETTING THE
LOVE THERMOSTAT

"There is nothing either good or bad,
but thinking makes it so."

— **William Shakespeare**

Over the years, I have learned that the brain is the most incredible gift we have, and it has the ability to continuously learn. This is why it is so crucial to understand how thinking works. In fact, it's not only through physical experiences that our brain changes, but also through our thoughts that we can reshape and evolve the structure of the brain in the same way we grow our muscles. For example, our earliest memories can have a strong influence on the development of our consciousness and can establish patterns of thinking that potentially shape our lives for better or worse. However, we have the power to override these patterns throughout our life. The way we interpret information determines where we place our attention and therefore also determines our intentions, and thus determines our actions. Therefore it is crucial to create the awareness that allows us to make conscious choices, and combine our attention with the willingness to endure the necessary effort to achieve our long term purposes.

Modern neuroscience has shown that the power to direct our attention toward specific subjects even has the power to shape our brain's firing patterns. This is why changing our thoughts and feelings can change our brain and, as a result, our lives.

A great example of how our thoughts change our brains can be seen through a study that scanned the brains of London taxi drivers, who are obliged to memorize all the street names of their city. The result of this study showed that these taxi drivers had thickened neural layers in their hippocampus, the region responsible for visual-spatial memories.

Similarly, research has proven that even through visualization we can change our brain structure. Athletes who train the repetition of certain movements, increase the thickness of specific areas in their brain linked to that movement. In his book, *How Your Mind Heals Your Body*, Dr. Hamilton notes that just by visualizing those movements on a regular basis, the same thing happens. He talks about a 2004 study at the Department of Biomedical Engineering at the Lerner Research Institute in Cleveland, which measured the increase of strength of thirty volunteers, of which some did physical training of their little finger, and others just imagined doing it. While those doing the physical exercises got stronger by 53%, surprisingly, those who only did the visualizations still increased their strength by 35%.

These insights are extremely empowering—especially if we add the fact that a certain part of our brain can't distinguish between reality and fantasy. This sounds incredible, but think about it for a second, why is it that we can watch a horror movie and feel frightened, although we know that it's only a movie, and that we're completely safe?

As conscious thoughts leave physical traces in the brain, and our brain can't separate fiction from truth, we can achieve unbelievable results through our ability to use our imagination. This is why it is important to fill our head with thoughts and positive feelings of being in a happy relationship. With each thought we repeat, we increase the connections between neurons and strengthen our new purpose.

With a fixed mindset, we lack the conviction that change is possible, and thereby allow our past to determine our future, as past experiences will have determined the purposes through which we interpret new events. However, once we become aware that we can reshape our mind and thinking, and develop a growth mindset, we give ourselves the choice to reset our inner thermostat by telling our brain what we want to think. We do this by creating a strong purpose of being in a fulfilled relationship, while removing past memories that are holding us back. In the second half of this book, I'll be discussing the steps you can take to engage with your thoughts, see them for what they truly are, and create new purposes and thought complexes that will let you take control of your life and achieve the goals you're aiming for.

PART TWO
A STEP-BY-STEP GUIDE
TO BEING IN A FULFILLING
RELATIONSHIP

*"A man becomes what he thinks
about most of the time."*

— **Thomas Emerson**

Now that we understand more about how the mind works, and how it can often work against us, we can begin to create the changes that will allow you to enter into positive relationships, and find the love of your life. These changes will not only help you to develop your relationships, but will also improve the quality of your life in general.

In the first part of the book, we discussed how we create invisible programs in our mind. These are created as a natural mechanism, and are one reason why the human race has developed so quickly in such a relatively short period of time. These automated programs allow us to perform many activities without spending much energy on them and also enable us to learn and progress.

The problem is that some of these programs can form an inner 'thermostat' that ensures we drift in a specific direction, which is not always where we would like to be headed. Once we notice and become aware that we're not achieving the results we desire, it is up to us to take responsibility and make a choice to change our course. We must reset our inner thermostat to promote the goals we seek. This can be difficult, as it entails a jump outside of our comfort zone. However, once a clear decision has been made, and is backed with our full engagement, change can happen much faster than we expect, opening the doors to joy and happiness. This has been my experience, at least.

As I mentioned earlier in the book, the catalyst for my change was being abandoned by yet another girlfriend. This is when I started my journey into personal development. The steps I took will be explained in the pages to come, but all of them focused on transforming myself and improving as a person, understanding why I thought the way I did and how I could change my thinking and my worldview to better represent the relationships I desired. I learned to be empathetic towards others, to not assume my first reactions were the ultimate truth of any situation, and to become more open and sharing. I began to understand what women really wanted: a man who was comfortable in his own skin, not a boy who was simply posing.

The impact of changing my thinking was a transformation of my dating life. While in the past it took lots of effort and nights of wild drinking to get dates, I was now suddenly attracting interest from girls easily and casually. I started visualizing being in a fulfilled relationship with the girl of my dreams, and noticed how gradually a whole cloud of shame that was stuck inside my head started to evaporate. It was as if I was finally giving myself permission to have a fulfilled life, and as if only now I granted myself permission to find the woman of my dreams.

I eventually met that woman in just as effortless a manner. A friend invited me to coffee and brought along a girl he had approached in the middle of the street. We instantly clicked. When this friend called me a week later for the number of a girl I knew, I asked him about his date from the other week, and he said they were only friends. So I gave him the number of the girl he wanted, and he gave me the number of the one I wanted. I texted her, and her response was ecstatic. We went to the same place we met, on our first date, and immediately fell for each other. Nine months later we were getting engaged on the beach, but none of this would have happened if I had not laid the groundwork within myself first. I had to change myself to become the right man, before I could find the right girl.

The aim of the steps in the rest of this book is to help you regain the ability to think and feel clearly (in the way that we do as children), which can be challenging at first. However, it is human to value most what we work hard for, and not the things we get as a gift. Therefore, I think it is not helpful to connect the concepts of *hard* and *bad*. Rather, we should develop our thinking skills to create a 'growth mindset,' with the belief that we can learn the skills we need and change in order to achieve our goals. Within this spirit, I can't imagine anything more rewarding than working on achieving the biggest reward of all: attracting a wonderful soul mate, and helping them to fulfill their life as well. Let's have a look at a step-by-step guide, which has allowed me to experience miracles in my life.

STEP ONE
DECIDE TO LIVE
YOUR DREAMS

"Life is either a daring adventure or nothing."
— **Helen Keller**

The first key to being in a happy relationship is to make a decision that you want to share your life with a partner and to become aware that being in a loving relationship is crucial to your happiness. This requires looking at the purposes you generally have in life and asking yourself if they are conducive to developing a happy, fulfilled relationship.

Since I was a teenager, I thought that I was pursuing serious relationships. For some reason, I was convinced I would find true love while being completely drunk in fancy nightclubs. However, one day I woke up, sick and tired of dating girls that continually broke my heart, and I made a decision to do whatever it would take to find a loving girlfriend. I realized that up until that day, I had felt attracted to the idea of having a gorgeous girlfriend, rather than actually being in a fulfilling relationship.

In *The Seven Habits of Highly Effective People*, Stephen Covey makes the important point that it isn't what happens to us that really matters, but how we respond. Therefore, in terms of relationships, it is critical to understand why we still have not attracted the love we deserve, and to become aware of the price we're paying for that failure. To do this, we need to lay down our pride and be willing to accept that we can always improve our life. We need to stop seeing ourselves as victims of circumstance, blaming others and justifying our life situation on outside forces beyond our control to avoid taking responsibility. This will be difficult for those of us who have received all their confidence from outside validation. Remember, for the vast majority of the time, the only thing responsible for our own personal success or failure is ourselves. However, short-term concessions will result in long-term happiness.

In my case, this realization happened once I understood for myself the pain of feeling unfulfilled. I became aware that I was not going to attract love without making a real change. I imagined aging on my own, lonely, and without any real love, as my parents would no longer be around. I sensed so much pain in that future situation that I made a decision to do whatever it would take to avoid it by finding a happy relationship. I accepted that I was making excuses for my previous failed relationships, and I promised to commit myself to seeing things the way they were, and not the way I wanted them to be. I realized I was bypassing the possibility of creating a life with meaning, where I could grow as a person together with my partner and create a real synergy.

By looking at the sport clients I was representing, I understood that the key difference between those who were successful and those who struggled lay in their decision to pursue their goals and delay instant gratification. Successful athletes live by the motto "hard is not necessarily bad," and enjoy pushing their limits.

I remember, for example, Novak Djokovic as a fifteen year- old player. Although undoubtedly talented, he was never considered the next big thing in tennis by anyone except himself or his parents. But he had made a decision to become the world's best tennis player and continuously pushed his limits to experience a happier and more successful life. And, when he was stuck at third in the world for a few consecutive years (behind Nadal and Federer), he understood that more was needed if he wanted to progress even further. So, he transformed his life, changed his diet, and worked on the mental aspects that would help him focus on becoming the best player in the world. He not only achieved the goal of reaching the number one spot in the world, but also now ranks among the greatest players of the modern era.

The 'marshmallow test' confirmed that the ability to delay gratification is a key predictor of success. In this experiment, scientists offered kids one marshmallow, or, if they could resist the temptation of eating it immediately, two marshmallows fifteen minutes later. The study found that those who could resist temptation and delay gratification would later become the more successful people in all areas of life.

Action Items:

Think of being in a happy relationship as much as possible

Think of your goal to be in a happy relationship on a daily basis, and contrast it to the pain of remaining single. Write out your goal every day, preferably in the morning, as if you had already achieved it. In my case, I wrote, *"I am in a fulfilled relationship with the woman of my dreams."* Generate feelings of excitement while you write this down. See if you can anticipate achieving this purpose, with all the feelings of joy and excitement that this would bring.

In personal development, consistency is an important key. Be careful not to give up or to falter in your determination to any degree. Think of this as less of a single action, and more of an ongoing process to keep your attention on frequently, rather than focusing on your previous, perhaps limited, expectations and outcomes.

Keep a reflective journal and track your emotions

Many singles I know have become numb toward most of their feelings. By tracking your feelings in a journal, you will gradually become more aware of them again. Remember, it is through emotions that we connect best with other people.

Ask yourself powerful questions

The quality of your life is related to the quality of the questions you ask yourself. Take a journal, ask powerful questions about your life, and be open to questioning past assumptions. Become a curious observer of your own life. These questions can include:

- Why am I still single? How were my past relationships?

- Why do I want to be in a relationship?

Good questions will allow you to witness the thoughts that form programs in your head, and which determine your behavior. Ask yourself:

- what if the answer my mind is giving me is simply a visible thought, rather than the deeper invisible thoughts.

We will come back to this issue below, but this is a good place to start.

STEP TWO
COMMIT TO A PLAN
AND BUILD MOMENTUM

---

*"The difference between a successful person
and others is not a lack of strength, not a lack
of knowledge, but a lack of will."*

— Vincent Lombardi

To achieve success, it is crucial to make a plan that includes your long-term goal of being in a happy relationship, as well as short-term goals you can achieve along the way. I did this by analyzing my life and defining where I wanted to be in a year. I brainstormed all the steps I would need to take to get from where I was to where I wanted to be, and I acknowledged that I would judge success by the effort I was putting into my personal journey, and not necessarily on the results.

In short, I created some clarity about where I was in life with regard to my vision of wanting to be in a lasting relationship. I'm giving you my blueprint of how I was able to turn around my life and attract the partner of my dreams. The key idea is that we attract the results that are aligned to our most prominent thoughts, which is why it is vital to create some understanding of our own psychology. This is why most of my steps can be practiced through the convenience of the cinema of our mind. I am convinced that by taking a decision to create a better life, by changing our belief system about ourselves, others, and life in general, we can accelerate change. This understanding is already becoming an important feature of other areas of life, like sport and business.

However, in addition to the steps in this book, I invite you to also think of other skills that you think could help you develop as a person holistically and which should, therefore, be part of your plan. For example, if you feel shy, why not try a drama or improvisation class for beginners? If you feel physically inhibited, salsa dancing could be a fun way to overcome this. If your attention is not steady, take up yoga or join a chess club. If you find talking to strangers awkward, go speed dating.

My point is, if you're aware that you're failing in one or more areas of your life (and let's face it, most of us are), it is the easiest thing in the world to ignore or accept it, avoid taking responsibility for it, and construct any number of excuses to keep things as they are and stick with the status quo. What you may not realize is that this failing will permeate all other areas of your life. If you do have insecurities about yourself or certain areas of your life that challenge you, now is the time to deal with them head on and finish them off.

People who have few insecurities or ungrounded fears, people who are confident and are happy being the center of attention (without actively seeking it out), are generally regarded to be more attractive. So take action now—make a complete list of the steps you want to take to change your life, number it in terms of priorities and sequence, then set timelines for all the tasks you have listed. Now take immediate action. Through daily action, you'll be taking a step toward success in achieving your main goal of finding true love.

The key is to stay committed to your self-development and to finding love. This means you devote yourself to your plan unreservedly. You do this by creating self-awareness and self determination to achieve the life you desire, by creating success habits. These success habits are crucial, so that you give yourself a clear message that you're working toward your biggest goal. Make sure you do them daily for at least thirty days, and continue to do them if you find they help you create a better life.

By creating success habits you will train your 'willpower muscles,' while also keeping energy expenditure to a minimum once the habits become automatic, so that you then have the mental space remaining to work on creating new success habits. Moving toward your goal and growing your willpower muscles simultaneously will give you more confidence and stronger self-esteem, which will motivate you to work even harder. You start feeling a sense of excitement as you witness progress and achievements, which allows you to focus on your positive developments, rather than any setbacks. Over time, you create a self-fulfilling prophecy to attract the love and life you desire.

The more habits you include in your life, and the more focused you are, the faster you will progress. Keep yourself motivated by linking lots of pleasure to your successes, and associating feelings of pain with a life devoid of a fulfilling relationship. Try to make all the actions of your plan as fun and enjoyable as possible, and make non-action painful. This is how you will create momentum and assured success.

Just one word of caution—be aware of 'bodyguards.' Once you enjoy new levels of success, you may feel tempted to take your foot off the pedal. This is your old self popping up again and trying to convince you that your old, easy life was just fine. These are your bodyguards showing up to try to remind you that your single life was fun, and that you don't need to endure the pain of change.

With every breakthrough, I experienced these bodyguards showing up in my life, either trying to slow me down, or to make me take on past habits again. However, by now you know that success habits are about more than just achieving particular goals, such as finding a date. They're about growing up and developing as human beings so that we can enjoy the most fulfilling life, and you achieve this by pushing your limits. Therefore, I urge you to thank your bodyguards for their input, but tell them that you will be continuing with the journey.

ACTION ITEMS:

Make a plan

Write down your goal and all the steps you could take to get there, without applying any sequence. Include the actions suggested in this book, as well as any success habits you feel could be helpful. Then prioritize all the actions you wrote down, and think of what skills you would need to successfully accomplish your tasks. Think also of who could help you learn the skills you need. Review this plan daily.

Take action and create momentum

Now take immediate action. Set some daily time in the morning and evening of each day to work on your long-term goals. Add new habits from your plan on a regular basis so that you're constantly adding firepower to your attempt to achieve your goal.

Monitor your progress

Make sure you're following through with your plan and adjust things if you don't witness the progress you anticipated. Starting this process is a big achievement in itself. Make sure you build momentum and prevent setbacks from throwing you off course. Notice when old habits pop up again in your life, but don't be too hard on yourself. With your new awareness, this will become easier.

STEP THREE
GET OUT OF YOUR HEAD

*"Do not dwell in the past, do not dream of the future,
concentrate the mind on the present moment."*

— **Buddha**

Before we start resetting our mental thermostat, it is important to give our head as much space as possible. This will help you find answers to the questions you're asking yourself, which is not possible when you're stressed and thinking very quickly. By relaxing, we allow our creative mind room to work, which helps us find solutions to our problems.

Slowing down our thinking makes it much easier to see our thought patterns, and to respond to our current reality, rather than relying on reactions based on childhood strategies that once served to protect us. It allows us to respond consciously to any situation. As Covey remarked, it is by slowing down the time between a stimulus and a response that we allow ourselves the time to make a conscious choice.

This step has been crucial to my personal development. My old self used to struggle with the many voices that would talk to me, from inside my own head, every time I encountered beautiful women. One voice would convince me that the girl I was talking to was not the kind of girl I would want to date. Another would tell me she was out of my league. A third voice was cautioning me not to fool myself. These voices hijacked my sense of humor, my spontaneity, and my true self, and really created a barrier to lasting relationships. By creating space in my head, my true self started to reemerge.

ACTION ITEMS:

<u>Meditate daily</u>

Start meditating on a regular basis. I started meditation by signing up to the free twenty-one-day meditation challenge of Deepak Chopra. Before my visualizations (see below), I would meditate daily, and I still do today. I started with five minutes but, after about a month, I was up to thirty minutes. Daily meditation was critical for me to create space in my head. I now use an application called Headspace, which is a different guided meditation series. I highly recommend these, as they have really made this practice a very easy and enjoyable daily habit. For more details, visit <u>allonkhakhsouri.com/free.</u>

<u>Solitude</u>

Spend time alone to think. I still do this every few days for at least an hour with nothing else to do but observe my thoughts. This was one of the most powerful practices I have adopted. Although it was extremely difficult for me at first to remain still, I became better at this each time I did it. I can now tell you that it is amazing how stillness can unlock so many stuck thoughts in our heads and give us answers we have been seeking for so long.

As I started to become more aware of my thoughts, I wrote in my journal some answers to questions that came to my mind while spending time in solitude. Over time, I also started to add longer walks in nature on weekends, or just spent time watching some nice scenery in order to calm my mind. Overall, these practices really helped me feel so much lighter in my head and in my life, as well as more energized.

STEP FOUR
CREATE A STRONG PURPOSE OF WANTING A RELATIONSHIP

"Imagination is everything. It is the preview of life's coming attractions."

— **Albert Einstein**

We all have purposes in our life that we pursue, whether consciously or not. If you're still single, it's because at some level this is what you want. Maybe being single gives you a feeling of security and stability, and the thought of allowing a new person to intrude into your life feels scary. However, the key to finding love is to create a purpose of wanting to be in a happy and fulfilled relationship. This means for many that we need to reset our 'love thermostat,' so that the idea of sharing our life with another person becomes fulfilling.

I created my long-term purpose by imagining myself being in the kind of relationship I desired, from the perspective of my own eyes and with lots of sense data. I envisioned clear pictures of spending time with my wife, experiences we would have, and how we would live a loving life together. I started doing this in great detail for a few minutes daily and, at one time, did this exercise for 10-20 minutes each morning, and 10 minutes each evening. It's incredible, but slowly my mind envisioned an intimate relationship as very pleasant and desirable. From the many steps I took to find love, this was possibly the most important one, especially now that I had created space in my head.

Please note there are four criteria that make such visualizations successful.

(1) The frequency of your visualizations—this will have an effect on how successful you will be in reforming your consciousness. The more you visualize, the better.

(2) The duration of your visualization—I used to do it for 10-20 minutes and at least twice a day.

(3) The intensity of your visualization—it is critical to attach many positive emotions to your visualization, and to sense the pleasure of being in a happy relationship while doing this.

(4) Finally, the vividness of your visualization—this stands in direct relation to how fast you will make your imagination become reality. Vividness means how clearly you see the images and pictures in your head while you visualize. The more details you see in your visualization, and the clearer those images and pictures are, the better.

ACTION ITEMS:

<u>Daily visualization</u>

Spend every morning visualizing. First, find a quiet location and then spend a few minutes to relax yourself through simple meditation. Simply place your attention on your breathing, and enjoy a relaxed state. Then spend 10-20 minutes visualizing being in a happy and fulfilling relationship. See yourself through your own eyes, being with the person you love, making each other smile, enjoying intimate moments together, and experiencing your daily life with your partner. Remember to use an active imagination and try to use clear mental pictures and impressions.

At first, this may seem difficult. Mental exercises can be difficult if you're not used to them, and your attention may wander. Just be patient with yourself and be disciplined. The key is to do this consistently, frequently, and repetitively on a daily basis, and not focus on the outcome in reality. Just remember, the greater the duration, frequency, intensity, and vividness, the more effective this exercise will be. Make this a daily habit and, if you can, do the same in the evening.

STEP FIVE
FREQUENT REPETITIVE THINKING

"You are today where your thoughts brought you. You will be tomorrow where your thoughts take you."

— James Allen

We are what we think, all of the time. This is how many successful athletes reach the state of believing they are successful before they have even competed. They think such thoughts during their preparation, and then they can perform with a state of mind where they believe they will win, no matter what. This gives an important mental edge to their performance. With this state of mind, whatever happens, they will compete to the very best of their ability.

Our conscious thoughts slowly transform our invisible thinking, or our subconscious, and therefore the totality of our lives. As discussed before, this is most significant to our development when we're young and our minds are less cluttered, far more malleable, and thus able to take on new information and change quickly. As adults, there is no reason, with the help of knowledge and self-discipline, that we can't go back to this childlike state of mind and begin to perceive life as it should be: simple and joyful.

Thoughts determine our beliefs and our expectations, which determine our actions, and eventually our habits and our experiences. So, the more we can reflect about the thoughts we want to have (about our life, ourselves, our relationships, our future, and so on), and the more we remove the thoughts that are preventing us from succeeding, the clearer our thinking will get. The easier it will then be for us to actually experience positive results in our lives from having consciously programmed these positive thoughts that are more conducive to happiness and fulfillment, rather than maintaining the ones that are contributing to our loneliness and stress.

We can do this with a tool called *frequent repetitive thinking*, which is like a mini-visualization. Frequent repetitive thinking requires us to spend thirty seconds, approximately ten times a day or more, thinking of the purpose we really want to achieve. It has two steps:

First step – we get ourselves to feel totally relaxed. A tool called 'going limp,' which I learned from The Kogan Academy, showed me how I could do this instantly. 'Going limp' involves disengaging and letting go of our current thoughts and becoming a passive observer of them. This concept, among other advantages, allows us to look at our thoughts, and therefore ourselves, objectively. We can then disengage from the thoughts that are not helping us achieve our goals and that we no longer want to think, and start to add in the thoughts that will help us.

To get into this mental state, we should, without any effort, simply think repetitively "I go limp." Imagine saying *I go limp* to yourself silently, then allow the perceived sound of these words to rise from your mouth, like smoke that is lighter than air, through the roof of your mouth, and into your mind. This image will help you to fill your consciousness with the correct impression of the thought *I go limp*.

Another image for 'going limp' that may help you is to imagine looking at a beautiful and serene river. Picture this exquisite river clearly and the peace and calm you get from it; then imagine a large piece of ugly trash floating past, spoiling your view. This piece of trash represents an unwanted thought. There is nothing you can do that will help improve this situation (i.e., getting stressed, upset, or frustrated) other than to sit and wait for the trash to float by, knowing full well that it will pass (as everything in life does). You can then return to enjoying the beauty of nature. This image should help you get into the important state of mind of 'going limp.'

The second step – while limp, includes another mini-visualization in which we picture ourselves in a happy relationship. Ideally, we do this with as much feeling and sense data of joy and pleasure as possible. In my case, I would literally catch myself smiling as I did this exercise. The more often we do this, the more effect it will have on our lives.

ACTION ITEMS:

Frequent repetitive thinking

You can do this anywhere and anytime, by just stopping yourself for a few seconds, making yourself feel totally relaxed for ten seconds, maybe 'going limp' first, and then using active imagination to visualize yourself in a happy and fulfilled relationship. This whole process doesn't take longer than thirty seconds and, ideally, should be done several times a day. Make sure to monitor that you do this exercise on a regular daily basis, as it is easy to forget. For example, I aimed to do this ten times a day, and would tick a box in my journal each time I did my visualization.

Silent sounds

Another tool from The Kogan Academy is called 'silent sounds.' 'Silent sounds' are conscious commands we give ourselves. I will explain how I use 'silent sounds.' First, I get myself into a very relaxed state for ten seconds by 'going limp.' Then I repeat to myself many times the command I want to give myself. The one I like best is "life is simple." As I repeatedly tell myself "life is simple," I imagine how everything in my life becomes light and easy.

In the same way as I described 'going limp,' sometimes I imagine saying the words "life is simple" and then picture the silent and perceived sound of these words rising through the roof of my mouth and filling my head with their sound. From this exercise, I develop a clear impression of life being simple and this feeling takes away lots of stress and anxiety that blocks me from being productive and accomplishing my goals. As life is really very simple, it is only our thinking that makes it confusing and complicated. I propose to do this a few times a day, as the whole process takes less than thirty seconds. I assure you that you will feel more relaxed and empowered.

STEP SIX
FIND A TRUSTED PERSON

"One man is no man."

— **Ancient proverb**

Leading neurologist V. Ramachandran researched the phenomena of anosognosia, which is when a deficit in self-awareness leads a disabled person to deny their physical limitations. He worked with patients who believed they could move their paralyzed arm. Ramachandran concluded that this form of denial is an expression of the adaptive defense mechanism of our left-brain hemisphere that attempts to protect the stability and well-being of our ego.

Fear- and shame-driven people will struggle to dedicate themselves to the truth, as their blocked emotions and unfinished thoughts bias their ability to see things clearly. Fear and shame create a tunnel vision through which we only see the truths that have served to protect us from pain. The beauty about being human though, is that we are imperfect beings. Coming out of hiding and sharing my innermost feelings and vulnerabilities was therefore a huge step toward finding love for me. Being able to share also prepared me for a loving relationship.

By expressing vulnerabilities, I learned to express my true self, which is what we all wish to do in our intimate relationships. I accepted that, as human beings, we are not perfect, and this allowed me to commit to growing and changing, which is best done with the help of a partner. Clarity often requires the help of an outsider to challenge the beliefs and habits that determine our behavior and tend to keep us within our comfort zone. Therefore, the single step of sharing thoughts and feelings with a non-shaming person, such as a therapist, an acting teacher, a family member, or a friend, can be the missing step to finding love.

ACTION ITEMS:

<u>Find a trusted person</u>

Choose a trusted person to share personal experiences and feelings with on a regular basis, and to help you with some of the actions that follow. Also, ask this person to hold you accountable to actions you plan to take in your quest to find a romantic partner.

STEP SEVEN
GET OUT OF YOUR DITCH

"We either make ourselves miserable, or we make ourselves strong. The amount of work is the same."

— **Carlos Castaneda Don Juan,** Journey to Ixtlan

We have discussed how our experiences, especially those from our childhood, which are now stored as thoughts in our minds, have influenced the creation of invisible patterns of thinking that really dictate how we currently live our lives. If we fail to become aware of these invisible thoughts, we will continue to live our lives in the same way in the future—regardless of what we consciously tell ourselves we want. To ensure the necessary changes to our thinking, and thus our success, we need to become aware of the often conflicting internal messages that are usually the result of these early memories. These may include feelings of shame and fear of failure or rejection.

These thoughts, usually the result of past experiences, give us such fear when we're young, that we cut them off to stop ourselves thinking about them, and to avoid any further suffering that we perceive these thoughts as bringing. For example, if a child is shouted at and smacked by their father for asking a simple, innocuous question, this experience may go toward developing an invisible thought in the child's mind that "people don't care" ("if my father doesn't care about me and ensure my understanding and proper development, then who will?")

Obviously, not all of our experiences and invisible patterns of thinking are negative. But the ones that are negative (and which result in stress, fear, suffering, and shame) are the ones that will continue to affect us badly until we address them and work on them in the correct way. Unfortunately, these unprocessed thoughts usually do remain unchallenged inside our heads, and often run our lives. Gradually, suppressed feelings of fear and shame become internalized memories in our nervous system, and shape part of our own identity.

Many people try to avoid facing these internalized feelings of fear and shame by seeking external validation. Robert Firestone talks about 'fantasy bonds' that many people have with drugs, alcohol, or sex. He argues that we all need true friendships, not these false *inhuman* idols. Other people suppress their fears and shame with pride. Again, this cover strengthens our invisible thought patterns and we continue to dig the ditch of our mind erosion ever deeper.

Through my work of sharing, I started becoming more aware of my interrupted thoughts and feelings. I discovered how I had created my own fantasy world that served to block emotions and thoughts from other people, as well as myself. My daily routines of meditation and spending time in solitude supplemented this work extremely well, as they helped me see the thinking that was causing my suffering and loneliness.

By working with my trusted people, I was gradually able to make visible the invisible thoughts that were preventing me from enjoying intimate relationships. I understood that I would need to finish off the thoughts that I was becoming aware of. Thoughts that, until now, I had never even realized I was thinking. These simple thoughts were the roots to a lot of stress in my life and to finish them off and get out of my ditch would be the beginning of a new era.

In self-help literature, we often read about reconnecting with our inner child, who has been lost for some time. I think this metaphor makes a lot of sense with many early memories. We are born as innocent, creative, and spontaneous kids. As we grow up, we experience a change. For instance, as children, we depend on our parents or main caregivers to survive, and this dependency can lead to developing a purpose of wanting to please the people we depend upon. This is when kids often feel the need to protect themselves by hiding their feelings, thoughts, and drives. Unfortunately, due to these inhibitions, we lose some of the spontaneous and creative traits we were born with, and we lose our freedom from ungrounded fears or neurosis. Yet, the traits that we lose are important for social interactions, so it is no surprise that it becomes harder for us to connect to people, especially strangers.

For example, many people attach lots of shame to our sex drive. There are many inputs to this—our parent's relationship to sex, religion, our society's viewpoint, our early sexual experiences. These can all be important elements that go toward the creation of 0ur invisible thinking about sex and result in thoughts like sex is lonely, filthy, frightening, disappointing, and so on. Feelings of shame attached to our sex drive are, of course, quite bizarre; without sex, the entire human race would become extinct within 120 years. By encouraging our inner child to grieve and to finish off the pains it wasn't able to express, we reconnect to our natural emotions, needs, and drives.

There are many different ways to do this. The method I learned from The Kogan Academy is called 'finishing off thinking' or 'foffting' for short, which simply means, *finishing off* our thoughts. Please note that I am only sharing here what worked best for me, and there are many different ways to deal with past events that are holding us back. 'Foffting' works by logically thinking through the thoughts that we had when we were young, past the point when they were interrupted by fear.

Let's look at the child who was struck by his father after asking him an innocent question, and subsequently grew up with the thought "people don't care." To finish this thought off, he would need to revisit this event in his memory and perhaps find out what his father was thinking about at that time. Perhaps the father was going through a particularly hard moment in his life. Once we start to understand people, it becomes easier to forgive and let go.

Talking with the father, without any malice, would also help to understand what the father really thinks. Did the child need to think, "People don't care?" Now he has more understanding and information about the event, and explore the issue of how this thought is also a reflection of his current circumstances. And we go on like this—finding answers to more and more questions, as our negative thoughts gradually weaken and get finished off.

How can we tell the thoughts that we were previously unaware of have been finished off? Well, we can talk and think about the events they relate to without any attached feelings of anger, self-pity, or shame. We can start to see that these thoughts are not a reflection of reality and that people are just people. Our stress levels improve and we become a lot lighter and happier, unburdened with thoughts we have been thinking based on events that happened years ago.

The process of 'foffting' is very good to do with a trusted person or a group (for more information on 'foffting,' see allonkhakhsouri.com/free), as you will start to see the similarities and affinities you have with others, how we are all very much the same, and this is reassuring. Of course, it can be done just as effectively on your own. To give an example, if someone had a terrible date, this may have been a very unpleasant experience. There is a good chance that person will have unfinished thoughts like "I'm a failure," "I'm inferior," "I won't ever find true love." If these thoughts are not thought through and finished off, they will continue to circle your head invisibly. By finishing off these thoughts, with all the sense data they come with, we take out the sting that such thoughts may have.

We can do this by tracing the thoughts to earlier experiences in which we felt the same sensations, probably feelings of helplessness or shame. By tracking earlier memories, we process any remaining charged energies that flow through our nervous system. These could be childhood experiences of feeling rejected or unloved. Once we have tracked our early experiences, and allowed ourselves to live through all the thoughts and feelings they may have triggered, we can then imagine ourselves reliving the same experience and responding in an appropriate and assertive manner. By doing so, we make sense of the past. This is how we can rewrite our life script, and our thoughts become empowering rather than limiting. We can also see and understand the purposes we had at the time that our invisible thoughts were created.

Finishing off your thinking will allow you to see the world as it is, not how you think it is, and this will give you the freedom to deal with any situation, in both your personal and professional life. By looking at the world with adult eyes, it became clear to me that past thoughts were no longer relevant to my life, and that I had the choice to ensure they would no longer guide me through my life decisions. This is a process that added to the quality of my life, but the key is to be patient. Finding a trusted person can make all the difference. For me, the one-on-one sessions with teachers from The Kogan Academy have been a game changer, as they helped me finish off the thoughts that were preventing me from finding a loving partner. If you would like to try a one-on-one session with The Kogan Academy teachers, please go to allonkhakhsouri.com/free to receive a promotional code for a free class

ACTION ITEMS:

<u>Work with your trusted person on finishing off your thinking</u>

I highly recommend you work with a trusted person and work through your thoughts and inner sensations. This person can be a one-on-one tutor from the Academy or, if you feel safe and comfortable, maybe a loved one. There are different ways of doing this, but the key is to make visible the invisible thoughts that prevent you from engaging in intimate relationships, and to think them through to their end.

The process of finishing off our thoughts works best by creating the conscious habit of asking valuable questions like: "What is bothering me now? What am I avoiding thinking about? How have these thoughts affected my life?"

The more we look at our thoughts and their attached felt sensations, and contemplate how our thinking has affected our lives and relationships, the easier it will be to re-experience and complete them in a manner that serves us well. This process may take time, as we have tried to cover up these thoughts and feelings for so long. Therefore, these thoughts may not want to reveal themselves easily—and will want to continue to exist even after we discover them. A starting point can be to validate past experiences that triggered fearful and shaming thoughts as real and acceptable. It can be an event as trivial as having feared to be left alone, but most of us will find more events that are more traumatic as well.

The very fact that you're sharing these experiences with a supportive person will make a huge difference. What helped me was to realize that what I was sharing were only my thoughts, and not who I was. My mentor made it very clear to me that every person has some weird thoughts that they keep for themselves. By externalizing feelings of fear and shame, and reliving past experiences in an assertive and appropriate manner, I was able to unlock my brakes and finally reprogram my 'relationship thermostat

For a list of some of the questions I went through with my acting teacher, visit allonkhakhsouri.com/free.

STEP EIGHT
CREATE A POSITIVE SELF-IMAGE

"A pessimist sees the difficulty in every opportunity; an optimist sees the opportunity in every difficulty."

— **Winston Churchill**

In the book, *How the Mind Heals the Body*, David Hamilton speaks about a wonder pill that can heal almost any disease. It's called a *placebo*. Research now shows that when we take a 'dummy drug' and believe it's real, the brain produces its own natural healing chemicals. Perception affects us so strongly that pharmaceutical companies often choose names for drugs that promote their perceived effects.

For example, Aaron K. Vallance suggests that the name Viagra sounds like Niagara and creates the perception of power. He challenges us to consider if the drug would have the same effect if it were called Flopsy. This is why it is critical to face life with a positive attitude, strong beliefs, and positive expectations. The way we see ourselves is reflected in the quality of our relationships. Therefore, it really is helpful to see ourselves as deserving of love and being worthy of the best possible partner out there. In fact, I believe how much we like ourselves, and to what extent we're willing to think positively about our lives and ourselves, will determine how well we will get along with others.

At the same time, it is also important to acknowledge that we all have our flaws—after all, we're only human. This is why it is crucial to see ourselves using what we have referred to before as a 'growth mindset.' A growth mindset allows us to see life as a learning process; loving ourselves and our partners no longer means we need to be or want to be perfect, but, rather, that we need to exert time and effort to progress in life.

A growth mindset also means that we accept setbacks and challenges as opportunities to learn. In fact, research reveals time and time again that a positive attitude is a key indicator for someone's success—the way we interpret events in our life will determine our destiny.

There are many ways to get inspired and strengthen our positive attitude. For example, I started reading lots of inspirational books, while also pushing myself to mimic positive role models who I admired. I also worked on overcoming limiting beliefs and replacing them with empowering ones. For example, I would write down my limiting beliefs, and describe the emotions they made me feel. Then, I would write down an empowering belief next to the limiting one, with the sensations that belief would make me feel. After I completed this list, I would read each limiting belief with the emotions I described with it, and contrast it with the empowering belief and its attached sentiments. I did this for several weeks, and instantly started focusing on beliefs and attitudes that would help me achieve my goals.

Another way to influence our attitude is by using our physiology. We spoke a lot about the importance of changing our thinking. But we can also influence our thinking through the way we behave. By acting the way we would like to see ourselves, we can jumpstart the inner changes we desire. For example, we can stand up straight, speak with a loud and clear voice, talk slowly, act relaxed and comfortable, and be detached from any outcomes. The aim here is to be our best self, radiate positive energy, and give pleasure and understanding toward the people we interact with.

ACTION ITEMS:

Change the inner voices in your head

Become aware of your inner dialogue and replace self-criticism, comparison, and judgment with positive, curious, and passionate self-talk. Speak positively toward yourself, and appreciate yourself, no matter what. I did this by saying statements like "I love myself" daily, and this has been surprisingly effective. To make such statements truthful, invest attention and time into yourself. You can do this by going to the gym, educating yourself, and having fun. In addition, spend time experiencing solitude regularly, meditating, and doing anything else that brings you closer to yourself. This is how you really get to appreciate yourself and recognize your true needs.

Allow yourself to make mistakes

The need to be perfect is what holds many of us back. If this affects you, it may be worth considering if wanting to be perfect is just a visible thought covering up an invisible counterpart that you perceive as being socially unacceptable.

It is important to allow yourself to be assertive and make mistakes by viewing them as a great learning opportunity. This is what makes us human. The tool of 'afterburning' (which we'll discuss in detail in step 10) allowed me to reset the concept of failure to a temporary setback, and thereby become fearless. As the famous inventor, Thomas Edison, once said before inventing the light bulb, "I have not failed; I've just found 10,000 ways that won't work."

Use the tool of 'afterburning' to learn, change, and grow positively. 'Afterburn' every day—looking back in mental pictures and impressions on your state of mind since you awoke, until the present moment. Ask yourself how your thinking affected your day, your relationships, your behavior, and think what purposes you had behind these visible circumstances—is this what you really wanted to achieve or just what you think you wanted to achieved? Think through the events of the day lightly, with a different state of mind, and see how this could have changed the circumstances. In doing so, you are positively restructuring your future. I also recommend that you 'afterburn' dates.

Act confident

Ask a friend to observe your behavior and observe what you could do to act more confidently. There are also a huge number of books about this subject, so I will only give a few suggestions:

- Stand up straight

- Talk with a loud and clear voice

- Talk slowly and make pauses

- Laugh freely and easily

- Be positive and don't take yourself too seriously

- Don't fiddle with your hands

- Be relaxed and comfortable during your interactions

- Be curious and pay attention to others

- Look people in the eyes when you talk

- Focus on speaking truthfully

STEP NINE
BECOME TRUE
TOWARD YOURSELF

*"It's not hard to make decisions if you
know what your values are."*

— Roy Disney

It is important that you discover who you are and express this in a relaxed manner, without trying too hard. Once you do this, it will become easy for you to interact with other people. Falling in love, in my experience, often happens when two people share similarities with each other. Therefore, it is essential to know the values that are important to you, and to live by them. By living in harmony with your values, you improve your self-image, confidence, and self-esteem. This is how you build character.

At the same time, it is equally important to know the values you are looking for in a partner—ideally, values that go beyond size and looks. Of course, physical attraction is important, however, I believe it is our personal commonalities that create real connections. When two people with similar values interact, they create a vibe together. Both sides feel comfortable to show who they really are and put their personalities on display. This vibe is what creates strong emotional bonds.

For me, it has been a great lesson to appreciate that people are still growing and developing, and that no one is flawless. Therefore, values can evolve and even change. Brendon Bouchard says in his book, *Charged*, that, in the end, every person asks themselves the same three questions: "Did I live?"

"Did I love?" and "Did I matter?" These are questions that highlight the value of personal development and growth, which are very dear to me. My fiancée shares these values, and I find it beautiful the way we encourage each other to continuously evolve ourselves.

I encourage you to include *growth* as one of your values. Another critical value for me is *integrity*. Integrity ensures we have 'clean contracts' with ourselves and other people—that is, we keep commitments, and we act in accordance with our moral values, so that we live up to being the person we want to be. By saying and living according to what you think and feel, people will start to trust and appreciate you. Eventually, they share the feelings that are boiling underneath their skin. The result of clean contracts will be that you will affect people on an emotional level, while making them feel very comfortable around you. This is very valuable in building comfort, trust, and attraction with new dates, girlfriends, and boyfriends.

Keeping clean contracts also includes our relationship toward ourselves. We need to respect ourselves, and not allow any form of abuse from other people. We do this by being assertive, and going for the things we want in life. It means setting ourselves high standards and doing what we can to achieve those goals. It also means being self-accepting, self-loving, and self-forgiving.

I urge you to be the kind of person who seeks the truth about yourself, your date, and about your relationships. I found that the more I became genuine, the more I enjoyed the presence of beautiful girls—until I found the one I wanted to share my life with. This reminds me of what Michael Jordan once said, "The harder I work, the luckier I get."

Having high values means you can really expect the best, and this includes aiming for the man or woman of your dreams. This might sound overwhelming at first, but remember that even the most desirable people are not looking for perfection.

Rather, they seek a genuine person who has clear values, a vision for their life, feels comfortable with occasional mistakes, and is honest enough to reveal their vulnerabilities.

ACTION ITEMS:

Think about your values

Define your values clearly in your journal, and those that you seek in a future partner. Ideally, review these values daily, and also incorporate these traits into your visualizations, imagining your husband or wife with both the physical characteristics that you feel attracted to, as well as the values and personality that you seek.

Although your values may change over time, it is critical that you know what you stand for and what you expect from a future partner. The clearer you are about what you want, the easier it will be to find it.

Create a vision

In addition, create a vision of where you would like to see yourself ten years from now. I did this in all areas of my life. I thought about where I wanted to be with regard to my health, fitness, career, income, relationships, emotional intelligence, education, skills, and spirituality. The clearer you are with your vision, the more attractive you will be to a future date.

Keep clean contracts

Commit to clean contracts toward yourself and others, and toward finding out the truth about yourself, your dates, and your relationships. Make integrity your master value, which ensures that you live in harmony with all your other values.

STEP TEN
CONNECT WITH YOUR HEART

"Everything that is really precious is right here, in our hearts. Everything is already right here."

— **Steven Glazor,** The Heart of Learning

Life is much more than the thoughts and stories we tell ourselves. By connecting to stillness, we connect to our true self. This stillness is the source of joy, love, and inner creativity, which can guide our mind to our true needs and desires. This is why slowing down our thinking and finishing off the unfinished thoughts that cause fear, stress, and suffering is so fundamental. It creates this space in our head. From here, we can start placing our attention on our heart, without being interrupted by our thoughts. And it is the heart through which we experience love.

Opening our hearts means exposing ourselves to vulnerabilities. By doing so, we also open ourselves up to love. This can be difficult, as many of us carry mental shields that once served to protect us during our childhood from pain and suffering. We have talked about this already. However, it is a practice worth pursuing, as these shields no longer serve us— the intimacy we desire requires the courage to be open and loving instead.

I was very privileged to grow up in Switzerland: a beautiful country, with very well behaved people, and a great education system have certainly contributed toward me living a great life. However, one other attribute I took on board from my surroundings was to show very little emotion, at least when sober. This may be the reason why Zurich seems like such a quiet and calm city during the day, but has one of the wildest party scenes I've ever encountered—when the people let their inhibitions drop, they have a lot of pent up emotions to express.

I discovered that I was living most of my life with a mask on my face, hiding my true self from others, and even from myself. In his book, *The Shame That Binds Us Within*, Bradshaw calls such behavior *human doing*, and not *human being*. To be ourselves, we need to grow up emotionally and accept all of our thoughts, feelings, and behaviors as part of who we are. We need to allow the inner child within us—who often felt abandoned, misunderstood, undiscovered, and unloved during our childhood—to reconnect to love and care. By doing so, we connect to our true self and to others as true human beings.

I have learned that we can access this loving part of ourselves by simply getting ourselves in a relaxed and still state, and then placing our attention on our heart. Once connected to our heart, we open ourselves up, and become honest, gentle, and loving. We're willing to express vulnerabilities, and to accept them in others. From here, we see things as they are, not as they pretend to be. To me, this is the place from which we can create true intimacy.

I must admit that for most of my life, I didn't allow myself to be open and vulnerable. This is what prevented me from forming intimate relationships. I used to think that exposing myself to others would be extremely painful. By gaining head space, however, I started appreciating myself for the way I was, and others for what they were. By accepting that we human beings are imperfect and vulnerable, yet unique and incredible, I was able to share very personal stories with women. They would instantly feel very comfortable with me and share their innermost secrets. This was a very strong bonding experience. By connecting to my heart, I also allowed my dates to experience the feelings that were boiling underneath their skin, and was able to touch them on an emotional level. My dates would feel connected with me in ways that they had never experienced before.

ACTION ITEMS:

Connect to your heart

Practice focusing your attention toward your heart. For example, during meditation, I would sometimes place one hand on my pulse and breathe in rhythm with my heart. Over time, I was able to sink into my heart during intimate moments with new dates, which allowed me to create real emotional connections. In this state, I became more open, loving, and forgiving, and was able to understand people's intentions instead of just their behavior.

Even today, I'm still a beginner at this, but just the awareness of these ideas has improved my life tremendously. The key to successful dating and relationships is ongoing work on our self, and connecting to our heart is a big step. You can practice this in everyday interactions with loved ones. At the same time, you will be opening your heart to love, and it will only be a question of time until you attract a fulfilling relationship. You will also instantly practice kindness, gentleness, and acceptance toward yourself and the loved ones you interact with

Love yourself unconditionally

Make a decision to love yourself unconditionally. This is a hard step for many of us. Love is work, so commit to that work, and do whatever it takes to accept every aspect of who you are. We may not be perfect, but we can learn and grow.

Making and keeping commitments related to your personal development will instantly increase your self-appreciation, while also improving your life. This is one way you can instantly increase your self-esteem and self-love.

Express yourself

Make it a habit to communicate honestly, and to express your needs and desires. As we have discussed many times, suppressing feelings can backfire in unpredictable ways. It is like pushing a beach ball under water—it will want to pop up again. In fact, being able to express ourselves completely openly is one of the beauties of a loving relationship. Until we achieve that relationship, it is important to do this with loved ones like parents, siblings, or close friends. If this is difficult, then we need to do it with a person such as a therapist. I know I'm repeating myself, but the single act of expressing ourselves very honestly could be your missing step to finding true love.

STEP ELEVEN
SOCIAL LEARNING

*"Much more genius is needed to make
love than command armies."*

— Ninon de l'endos

In the 1990s, Italian neuroscientists under the leadership of Giacomo Rizzolatti observed that particular motor-command neurons are fired in the brains of monkeys when they execute certain activities, and that these same neurons are also fired when they observed other monkeys doing the same activity. These 'mirror neurons' allow monkeys to imagine themselves doing something they observe, and enable us humans to go even further. We have the ability to place ourselves inside the minds of others, and even imagine what they're thinking. This is how we're able to fully understand people, and empathize with what they're going through.

Through these skills, our ancestors could cooperate to a very high level. Meeting a partner and creating relationships requires similar social skills, as communication is our bridge to interactions. Many people fear that they will run out of things to say, and this can become a big obstacle in our dating lives. But, in fact, communication can become very easy if we develop true curiosity to listen to and understand the person we're speaking with.

I always noticed that there were people who easily attracted partners and continuously enjoyed relationships, while others kept struggling to find a partner. I considered myself a smart person, and a good person, and I was certainly experiencing lots of amazing moments in my life. After going through many of the previously mentioned steps, I also finally felt much more

100

comfortable with dating outside of my comfort zone of nightclubs.

Nevertheless, I still didn't sense that I was really connecting to women on a deeper level. What opened my mind was the realization that there is something called emotional intelligence, which consists of the kind of human skills that enable certain people to develop more meaningful relationships. Those people are more engaged with themselves, and with the people around them. Somehow, our educational systems seem to skip this important subject that teaches a life skill we should all possess.

Being able to develop deeper connections gives us an amazing platform to get to know a partner better than most people ever have. I began to focus on understanding what motivated and inspired the girls I was speaking with, and this led to many amazing conversations. I realized that speaking about topics that evoke feelings and passion, like childhood experiences, future dreams, hobbies, and passions, as well as relationships themselves, allowed me to dig deeper than was usual during dates. Once your date gives an answer, try to really relate to them by making an attempt to understand who they are. Imagine what it's like being them, and show real interest in their motivations. Using these simple ideas resulted in girls telling me how I understood them better than their previous boyfriends did.

At the same time, it is important to reciprocate and share personal stories and even vulnerabilities. I noticed that when I would express sincere feelings as part of my stories, they immediately became a powerful way to create a deep connection between my date and myself, as sharing is truly bonding. Sharing empathy is what I believe creates a bubble that links two hearts together.

I encourage you to be the kind of person that radiates positive energy, and who gives pleasure and understanding toward the people you interact with. One tip I have for great conversation is to include lots of imagery and emotion in your language, and make assumptions from time to time. Be like a curious child. Think in pictures and impressions, without any stress or thinking about the outcome. This will naturally lead to spontaneous conversations.

For example, if your date mentions that she just came back from New York, you can describe how you can picture her bringing the whole city to a complete standstill as she exits a cab with all her millions of shopping bags and gifts that she bought for all her friends. You can also tell her that she seems like the kind of person who loves adventurous trips. The key is to create these magic moments between two people that become so connecting. To help get into the right state, use 'foreburning' (which we'll be discussing in a few pages) as a way to prepare your state of mind for events such as dates.

ACTION ITEMS:

<u>Work on the skills you feel you need to improve</u>

Remember, we're human and, as humans, we don't need to be perfect. At the same time, it is always great to grow and develop new skills. Therefore, work on becoming a person anyone would want to meet again after a date. Make sure you'll be a good conversationalist and listener who always has something fun and interesting to say. Mix deep subjects with fun and amusing stories, and evoke different positive emotions like excitement, attraction, and curiosity. Also, live the kind of exciting and adventurous life any date would want to be part of. And use every opportunity to show that you really understand who they are and what they enjoy.

As I've mentioned before, this is the beginning of a journey of positive change within yourself. If we can work on developing ourselves as people, and thus become more compassionate, energized, understanding, and happy as an indirect result, we will attract the partner that fulfills our desires.

Become a good listener

By listening to a partner, and empathizing with what they say, you instantly create attraction. In fact, as I love to interrupt, I made it a habit to not say a word while my date was speaking and wait another few seconds once she was done before responding. Sometimes, I would rephrase what she said before giving my input and, whenever relevant, express empathy with what she said.

I would literally imagine myself in her situation, understand what she was experiencing and desiring in that moment, and only then respond. I understood with time that even the most attractive women felt insecurities and fears, which they tried to cover up. By learning to listen to women's words and body language, I started to appreciate people much better, and this helped me connect with girls on a much deeper level.

Be curious about your dates

Be genuinely curious and interested in your date, and find out what their story is. Ask good questions, so you understand them as a deeper being. You should soon know why they do what they do, what their dreams are, and what their best childhood memories were, to name just a few examples.

STEP TWELVE
HAVE COURAGE AND FUN

"I will not learn about fire by thinking about fire but by burning."

— **Carla Needleman,** The Work of Craft

As I believe it's a man's duty to initiate most interactions, this chapter might seem more relevant to men. Nevertheless, I do believe techniques like 'foreburning' are extremely useful for everyone, and I will be explaining these below in more detail.

It's important to always remember that meeting people should be fun. It is therefore crucial that you associate pleasure with meeting people, while looking at less successful interactions with humor and curiosity, so that you can learn what went wrong. I can assure you that, based on my experience, you will meet many new men or women once you start following the steps in this book. However, make sure you spend time in places where you can actually meet the kind of people you're interested in. This could be by taking up a new hobby, going to yoga classes, going clubbing, or meeting people on the streets and in the midst of your daily life. Then make sure you become familiar and comfortable with the setting, so that you start meeting new people.

For example, I always dreamed of having the ability to meet girls during the daytime and in the midst of my normal life—it made me suffer to see girls I liked and just let them walk by. This is probably the hardest way of meeting girls, and yet it can become quite easy. I am briefly mentioning this here, as these skills are so related to what goes on in our head.

It took me some time until I was able to build up the courage to speak to random girls in the middle of the day. However, I was inspired by other friends I knew who did this successfully, and with remarkable results, and I really wanted to be like them. So, I started 'foreburning' how I would do this, and how I would deal with the anxiety I felt each time I saw a girl I liked on the streets.

Eventually, I found out the big secret, and pushed myself to approach girls. The big secret was being truthful about my intentions and my drive to meet girls, while remaining curious and interested in the girl I was speaking to. I quickly realized that if I was genuine, and told the girl exactly what I was thinking, they would usually feel quite flattered. By being curious and interested, I also had no problem keeping the conversation alive and fun.

I now know that most single girls dream of meeting their Prince Charming completely out of the blue in the middle of the day. The key is to approach them without any hesitation, capture their attention, tell them in all honesty, and in a slow and relaxed pace, what you're thinking. By giving someone a courageous compliment in the middle of the day, you're genuinely adding value to their life, which gives you instant plus points. I have met some of the most amazing girls in the most regular places, like tubes (subways), lineups, or simply on the street.

My point here is that there are natural social skills that fit well into any environment, and we can learn them, once we master the skills of thinking. I encourage you to become a social scientist, find out what works, and why it works. Watch people, read books, and do whatever helps. Just be genuine, have fun, and add value to the people you interact with. This demonstrates the values of honesty, spontaneity, courage, and drive, which most people find attractive. This will ensure that you will meet and connect with lots of others.

Of course, approaching people can seem scary at times. Being afraid makes us human. In fact, girls will forgive a bit of nervousness, as it shows you don't approach girls for a living. However, I want to propose a few tools that really helped me transform fear into courage, and I highly recommend you use them daily, and especially before important events, such as dates.

The first tool – is called 'foreburning.' 'Foreburning' is a technique I learned from the acting school where actors prepare themselves for a role by using an active imagination and playing the full scene in their head. It's a method that can help prepare us for any event. This could, for example, be done before any kind of interaction with a very attractive girl or boy.

In these situations, we often have an increased intensity of thinking, including fears that something could go wrong. This triggers anxiety. Remember, if you have this anticipation and resistance to meeting and talking with attractive people, this fear is a result of an ungrounded thought you're thinking irrespective of the circumstances (you don't know what the girl will be thinking, but if you anticipate what she will be thinking, and these projected thoughts can become a self-fulfilling prophecy).

As discussed, these ungrounded fears you have now are a result of invisible thoughts that you have about yourself and your life that you need to engage with and finish off. Past experiences that have created an invisible generalized thought like "women are frightening" or "I'm worthless" create nerves, anxieties, and resistance to action.

It is important to note that these fears are based on exaggerated evaluations of the past, as we know that nothing too terrible can really happen on a date. At worst, messing things up leads to some amusing stories to share with friends. However, by preparing ourselves and anticipating an enjoyable interaction, we set ourselves up for successful experiences.

For example, I would use 'foreburning' to visualize dates, by picturing myself just before meeting a hot girl, being nervous, and then slowly calming myself down, going on the date, having an amazing time, and handling every situation successfully. I would use my active imagination to create the impressions and thoughts I would want to have while on the date, including the state of mind I wished to be in. This would also include handling moments of tension and awkwardness, and feeling myself stay calm and relaxed. My 'foreburn' would last several minutes, and I would usually do it within an hour before a date. In a sense, it served as a rehearsal to my date.

The second tool – is called 'afterburning.' 'Afterburning' is a tool you can use after events such as dates. Once an event is finished, the intensity of our thinking decreases. However, we still have unfinished thoughts circulating our head. By 'afterburning' the event, we run through the entire experience and are able to dissipate the remaining thoughts from the date, including negative ones, rather than just suppressing them. As a result, we benefit from lots of feedback that will help us act in a relaxed manner on future dates. 'Afterburns' also help us learn from our experiences, so we can have better experiences in the future. This is how I turned my mistakes into very valuable lessons.

'Afterburns' also helped me overcome sticking points and to learn from challenging moments. For example, I noticed that after successfully opening a conversation with a girl, I would often hit a dead end. Although the girl seemed to enjoy my approach, she still didn't give much input into the conversation. I noticed that *I* had to find a way to keep the conversation alive until the girl was comfortable enough to engage in it as well. So, over time, I learned a nice technique whereby I would make a few creative assumptions, which would both make her smile and get her to interact instantly. This happened thanks to the thinking I did when 'afterburning' interactions I had.

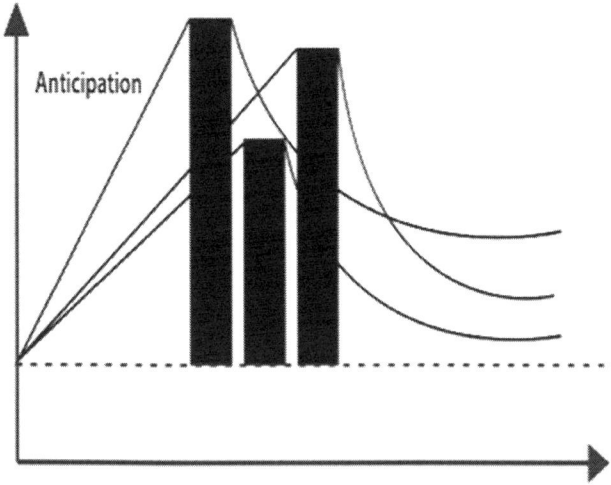

Figure 6: Unfinished thinking becomes background noise. Notice how, after the event, the thinking does not reduce down to zero, but continues at a level relative to the original importance of the thought (adapted from Sam Kogan, The Science of Acting)

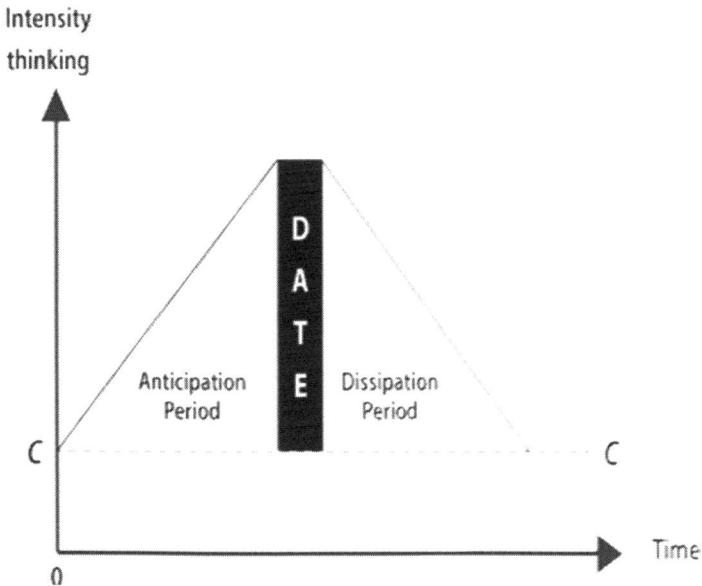

Figure 7: 'Foreburning' and 'afterburning' a date. This is how we can anticipate an event free from fear, and finish off any unpleasant thoughts after the event. You should note that the intensity of the thoughts dissipates back down to the same level as the pre-date period (adapted from Sam Kogan, The Science of Acting).

'Foreburning' and 'afterburning' are excellent tools that I now use before and after any intensive event, including business meetings or personal confrontations. Sometimes I use a third tool, 'going limp,' before doing my 'foreburns' and 'afterburns,' to get myself instantly in a relaxed and calm state. 'Going limp' is a way to allow a thought to be there, without repressing it. It can be used anytime we know we have a thought that is not good for us. I do this by picturing myself under a nice pleasant shower, which suddenly turns ice cold. While this happens, I focus on relaxing myself and simply bearing the ice-cold water as it splashes all over my body.

By the way, I mentioned how I wanted to master the skills of being able to talk to random girls that I liked in the midst of the day. This might sound difficult, and attracting love shouldn't be difficult once we set our love thermostat right. Funnily enough, I ended up meeting my fiancée without any heroic actions.

Instead, we met through a friend, who did the hard work for me, and who had met her in the middle of the day on a busy road! This is what I call the law of attraction. I was ready for love, worked hard on myself, and then the woman of my life was served on a golden platter.

ACTION ITEMS:

Meet people and have fun

Find the environments where you can meet new people and feel comfortable. Make sure you actually meet others on a regular basis. Set goals and hold yourself accountable! Keep a journal if you need to, to ensure you're progressing gradually. If you feel shy, start by making it a goal to casually speak with people, ask genuine questions, and gradually build the interaction. For example, the goal in week one could be to speak to a handful of men or women, while a few weeks later it might be to get phone numbers and dates. The key is always to move forward, learn from setbacks and use them as feedback, and stay focused and positive.

Get into the right state and use the tools of 'foreburning' and 'afterburning'

I also recommend you make approaching and talking to people fun, in whatever setting it is. Get in the right state before meeting others, regardless of whether it's a date or a social setting. Using physical activity helps us to feel in a good and alert mood. Use the techniques of 'foreburning,' 'afterburning,' and 'going limp.' Try to smile genuinely whenever you can and find the right vibe for the person you're interacting with.

STEP THIRTEEN
TRAIN YOUR WILLPOWER
MUSCLE AND TAKE ACTION

*"Something in human nature causes us to start
slacking off at our moment of greatest
accomplishments. As you become successful, you will
need a great deal of self-discipline not to lose your
sense of balance, humility, and commitment."*

— H. Ross Perot

Prominent American executive Claude C. Hopkins wrote in his autobiography, *My Life in Advertising*, that the key of his success was to induce new habits in potential customers. He explained that a habit consists of three parts: a clue, certain routines, and rewards. For example, when he promoted a new toothpaste called Pepsodent in the early 20th century, most Americans didn't brush their teeth. So he created clues that reminded them of a 'black film' around their teeth and promised the reward of white teeth if they used Pepsodent. In addition, Hopkins invented a cool and tingling sensation that customers would enjoy with the new toothpaste. The idea was that the absence of that sensation made customers remember that they had forgotten to brush their teeth.

Hopkins argued that with the right clue for a new routine, combined with a reward and a craving, we could teach customers any new habit. The clue of loneliness and the craving for a better life with the woman of my dreams inspired me to work on myself. The tingling sensation was the growing success I enjoyed in every area of my life, almost instantly— with the ultimate reward being my wife.

We have already discussed that the biggest obstacle to change is our self-image. The way we see ourselves directly affects whether we think we're able to evolve to become a person that attracts what they desire. It also determines what kind of partner we feel we   deserve. Therefore, we're often subconsciously programmed to postpone changes in our life. By making and keeping commitments, we shift our self-image. We demonstrate that we can change our life, and this in itself changes our self-image. Therefore, willpower is the master key to any success.

The critical difference between successful people and unsuccessful people comes down to a few habits, done on a regular basis. By introducing success habits, we immediately turn our life in the direction of progress and growth. At the same time, we also train our most important muscle, the 'willpower muscle.' Willpower needs to be worked out, trained, and spared from using its energies on useless tasks. This is why it helps our willpower when we take care of ourselves and feel energized and rested. After an initial pain period, we create automatic actions that become easier over time and direct us toward our goals, and this allows us to work on new challenges.

What holds most people back is procrastination. This is why we often stay within our comfort zone and justify this with excuses. By creating new habits, we can reset our inner thermostat, and we can do so for every area of our life. I did this by following the actions in this book, as well as adding other positive traits—waking up early, no drinking at parties, and going to the gym. I combined my long-term goal of finding a wife with short-term goals of personal wellbeing and effectiveness.

The first challenge is to start with a new habit, and the second one is to continue following through with it and building momentum. Persistence is crucial. One obstacle is self-sabotaging behavior: for many, the fear of failing to attract a girlfriend or boyfriend and the humiliation of rejection is why they don't really try their best to be in a relationship. This can even result in odd behavior, like going after unobtainable girls or boys, or taking actions that make failure inevitable.

Research has shown that students studied much less for an exam when their studying times were recorded —whereas normally they could have made the excuse that they didn't study much if they failed the exam, they were now concerned that if they studied hard and still failed they would have no excuse. Consequently, to give themselves an excuse for failure, they simply didn't study as much.

This form of self-sabotaging sounds absurd, but when we start to see how prevalent the purpose of wanting to fail is among us all, this behavior is understandable. By wanting to fail, we miss out on the opportunity to make our dreams come true and to build our self-esteem, confidence, and happiness. As it can be difficult to see and acknowledge self-sabotaging behavior, it is very helpful to have a non-shaming and trustworthy person with whom we can share our personal experiences. This person can help you make sure that you won't be afraid of short-term setbacks, nor care what people think of you.

In my case, I remember, I used to hide the fact that I wanted to be in a relationship. In hindsight, I believe I tried to escape any kind of pressure by making it seem as if I wanted to be single. Of course, this was invisible thinking, and I wasn't aware of it at the time. Of course, by focusing on this, I made being single an unavoidable reality. Once I started to become mindful and more aware of my thinking, began to work on it, and enjoyed the support of my mentors, I went to the opposite extreme: I announced to all my friends that I was working on myself, and that I wanted nothing more than to have a girlfriend in the near future, which inevitably became a reality. Surprisingly, my friends all respected me for expressing my intentions so courageously.

I highly recommend you hold yourself accountable to your success habits and find ways to ensure that you're progressing. This can be through assigning a mentor to work with you, announcing your intentions to the whole world, or giving yourself continuous reminders.

ACTION ITEMS:

Train your 'willpower muscle' with short-term goals

The easiest way to train your 'willpower muscle' is by creating new success habits that, in time, become automatic processes. I propose you choose a few habits that will serve your general well-being and efficiency. These can include waking up earlier, going to the gym regularly, making 'foreburning' and 'afterburning' an involuntary habit, doing 'silent sounds' daily, or drinking less at social events.

Remember, every success habit is hard to begin but, after about a month, they become automated processes. By creating new success habits, you not only improve your life, but you build up confidence and self-esteem, making success a self-fulfilling prophecy. Make sure you persist, but also be forgiving of yourself if you don't manage to follow through, and then just start again.

As your 'willpower muscle' grows, it will become much easier to introduce new habits, and you can replace negative ones that are harming you.

Create success habits related to finding love

Use the actions in this book to create your routines for attracting people. Make sure you develop the skill of having clear thoughts related to the purpose of being in a fulfilling relationship. Look for and start to finish off the thoughts that create obstacles in your mind to the purpose of wanting to be in a happy and fulfilling relationship. Again, if you're having challenges with this, re-read the relevant chapters in this book and watch the videos for more information. Start with one and make sure you follow through for at least thirty days so that the conscious habit becomes automatic. Gradually add new ones, until you're implementing all the key action points I describe in this book.

Once you have a handful of new habits, you can join them together into success routines. These can be morning routines when you wake up, evening routines before you go to sleep, or routines before dates and other stressful events. With these new routines, you create a new lifestyle, while also strengthening your willpower. Eventually, your routines will all work in tandem with each other and create the self-fulfilling prophecy of success and happiness.

Make it a habit to step out of your comfort zone

Once you feel stronger, make it a habit to step out of your comfort zone. I did this by making it a rule to dance in clubs, give toasts at events, and approach girls on the streets. Have your own rules, and make sure you follow through. Go after what you fear, like talking in front of people at public events, or introducing yourself to someone you find attractive.

STEP FOURTEEN
BECOME UNSTOPPABLE

"To achieve something you have never achieved, you have to become someone you never were before."

— Les Brown

This journey is not so much about learning tricks to find the partner you dream of, but becoming a person who attracts love, and is then able to hold on to a partner and experience the kind of life together that wouldn't be possible alone. Initially, the willingness to accept change was a difficult step in my life. However, over time, it became part of my vision to strive to grow and evolve as a human being.

Within this context, finding love is only the starting point to a more fulfilling life. Learning to lead a meaningful life in which both partners contribute to each other's spiritual growth and personal joy is the true gift and the trait we nurture through this journey. For most singles, their conditioned actions are what makes it harder and harder to step out of their comfort zone and take the actions that would fulfill their desire of creating a lasting relationship.

The law of inertia refers to the resistance of any physical object to any change in its state of motion. Without outside intervention, the object will continue moving (or not moving) in the same direction. I hope this book will be the outside intervention that will inspire you to change your direction, so you can attract the loving partner you deserve, and continue doing the things that will enhance the quality of your life. The key is to get started and keep going.

I'm convinced everything people do is ultimately done to find happiness and love, at least on an invisible level. So, if you're not attracting the kind of partner you desire, you may be setting your 'love thermostat' at a level that would keep you safe from the unpredictability of intimacy. This is because, for reasons that you will need to consider and engage with, your brain thinks you are happiest by yourself and need to be protected from outside intruders. You may resist your 'bodyguards,' but your inner thermostat will always bring you back to the comfort zone of your safety level. This can be in the form of keeping you away from men or women, attracting incompatible partners, or simply by turning existing relationships into a living hell.

However, as you now know, we can change this predicament. By setting compelling goals, like finding fulfilling love, and by taking action on these goals, we set a new course for our life. We do this by creating the mental equivalent of what we want in our lives, and reconnecting to our instinctive drive. It's like unpeeling the layers that protect a fruit. By unlearning conditioned thoughts and behaviors, we reset our 'love thermostat' back to its natural settings, and allow love to flow into our lives. We form the consciousness and authentic character that allows us to attract the love we seek.

Training your mind is the most important skill you can work on. Your thoughts and beliefs affect every facet of your existence even on a cellular level. The way we interpret events will determine the actions we take, and the fate we attract.

The key, in my view, is to make finding a companion your most important goal for the coming year. Structure your life so that the things you want will happen. Set conditions that will increase your odds of sticking to new habits so that outcomes you want will happen automatically. Have a mentor who can keep you accountable. Stay fully engaged with this challenge, your development, and your life. And, most importantly, have faith in yourself and this journey. Once you embark on this road, trust the process and let go of any expectations. As paradoxical as it sounds, creating clear intentions and then letting go of expectations has been the secret mix that allowed me to prosper so quickly. So enjoy the process and don't depend on the outcome, as your desired results will unfold once you're ready.

The process of finding love will give you lots of joy, as you will experience how you're growing as a human being. For me, this process was about growing up from being a needy boy to becoming a real man, a creator who gives and receives. I learned through the challenge of finding a partner the knowledge that I have shared with you, to raise my emotional intelligence and create the thoughts and feelings that serve me. From here, it became inevitable that I would attract the woman of my dreams, as I was able to create deeper connections and become a fulfilled person.

Ultimately, I believe this is a journey of personal development, and that is what I think life is about. Through personal growth, you will not only begin to attract the people you're attracted to, but also the person you appreciate the most. Through personal development, life will become ever more joyful and fascinating. I urge you to take action, by introducing the ideas in this book and creating success habits. I wish you good luck, and I look forward to hearing about your journey.

ABOUT THE AUTHOR

Allon Khakshouri is a Swiss and Israeli entrepreneur and lawyer, who also has a Masters in Diplomacy and Conflict Resolution. Allon has been involved in sports for most of his adult life. He has managed some of the best tennis players in the world, and accompanied current world number one, Novak Djokovic for over 8 years, as his exclusive agent. In addition, he has been involved in the organization of various events and is on the Council of the Association of Tennis Professionals.

Allon has always been intrigued by what makes some athletes more successful than others, and in particular the impact of the mind with regards to success in both sports and other areas of life. He has been researching the secrets of breakthroughs over the last few years, and you can find more information on his blog at www.allonkhakshouri.com.

FREE GIFTS FOR READERS

Throughout this book, there are numerous mentions of additional resources that can help you through this journey. You can find all of these, as well as exclusive video interviews and get access to Allon by visiting:

AllonKhakshouri.com/free

Bibliography

- *The Science of Acting*, Sam Kogan
- *Focus: The Hidden Driver of Excellence*, Daniel Goleman
- *Mindsight: The New Science of Personal Transformation*, Daniel J. Siegel
- *Healing the Shame That Binds You*, John Bradshaw
- *Change Your Thinking, Change Your Life*, Brian Tracy
- *Hardwiring Happiness*, Rick Hanson
- *True Happiness: Your Complete Guide to Emotional Health*, Dr. Mark Atkinson
- *Why Kindness Is Good For You*, David R. Hamilton Ph.D.
- *How Your Mind Can Heal Your Body*, David R. Hamilton Ph.D.
- *Conscious Living: Finding Joy In The Real World*, Gay Hendricks
- *The Charge*, Brendon Burchard
- *Awaken the Giant Within*, Anthony Robbins 203
- *Authentic Happiness,* Martin E. P. Seligman, PH.D.
- *What's Stopping You*, Robert Kelsey
- *The 7 Habits of Highly Effective People*, Stephen R. Covey
- *Maximum Willpower*, Kelly McGonigal
- *Mindset: The New Psychology of Success*, Carol S. Dweck
- *My Life In Advertising,* Claude C. Hopkins

ACKNOWLEDGEMENTS

I want to thank all the people who have helped me with my personal life journey. Of course, without my parents and their guidance, I would not have evolved to become the person I am now. I want to thank the many women I have known throughout my dating years, who all have taught me valuable lessons about life and myself. My many friends who have always supported and encouraged me in all my endeavors. Many thanks to my mentors, Elizabeth Bowe and Luke Eppel, Neil Sheffield, the director of The Kogan Academy, and all their amazing teachers—they have literally changed my life. I want to also thank Erlend Bakke, who inspired me to write a book; Steven Heywood for editing this book; Luanne Thibault for proofreading; to Austin Netzley and Joe Shaffer to help me make this book possible; Genesis Canedo for the artwork; James Amora for setting up the website; and to my friends who gave me valuable feedback. Last but not least, I want to thank my wife, Naomi, who has opened the doors to a new level of joy and happiness and who is the light of inspiration in my life.

Printed in Great Britain
by Amazon.co.uk, Ltd.,
Marston Gate.